The History of Conservation
Preserving Our Planet

Wind, Waves, and the Sun
The Rise of Alternative Energy

Cathleen Small

New York

Published in 2018 by Cavendish Square Publishing, LLC
243 5th Avenue, Suite 136, New York, NY 10016

Copyright © 2018 by Cavendish Square Publishing, LLC

First Edition

No part of this publication may be reproduced, stored in a retrieval system, or transmitted in any form or by any means—electronic, mechanical, photocopying, recording, or otherwise—without the prior permission of the copyright owner. Request for permission should be addressed to Permissions, Cavendish Square Publishing, 243 5th Avenue, Suite 136, New York, NY 10016. Tel (877) 980-4450; fax (877) 980-4454.

Website: cavendishsq.com

This publication represents the opinions and views of the author based on his or her personal experience, knowledge, and research. The information in this book serves as a general guide only. The author and publisher have used their best efforts in preparing this book and disclaim liability rising directly or indirectly from the use and application of this book.

All websites were available and accurate when this book was sent to press.

Library of Congress Cataloging-in-Publication Data

Names: Small, Cathleen, author.
Title: Wind, waves, and the sun : the rise of alternative energy / Cathleen Small. Description: New York : Cavendish Square Publishing, [2018] | Series: The history of conservation : preserving our planet | Includes bibliographical references and index. Identifiers: LCCN 2017029855 (print) | LCCN 2017032808 (ebook) | ISBN 9781502631336 (E-book) | ISBN 9781502631329 (library bound)
Subjects: LCSH: Renewable energy sources--Juvenile literature.
Classification: LCC TJ808.2 (ebook) | LCC TJ808.2 .S63 2018 (print) | DDC 333.79/4--dc23
LC record available at https://lccn.loc.gov/2017029855

Editorial Director: David McNamara
Editor: Kristen Susienka
Copy Editor: Rebecca Rohan
Associate Art Director and Designer: Amy Greenan
Production Coordinator: Karol Szymczuk
Photo Research: J8 Media

The photographs in this book are used by permission and through the courtesy of: Front cover, Yangphoto/E+/Getty Images; p. 4 Steve Proehl/Corbis/Getty Images; p. 6 Joseph Sohm/Visions of America/Digital Vision/Getty Images; pp. 8-9, 42 Panoramic Images/Getty Images; p. 10 Janek Skarzynski/AFP/Getty Images; p. 12 Moehri, own work/File: Möhrendorf Wasserräder Schmiedsrad.jpg/Wikimedia Commons; p. 15 Joseph Sohm/Shutterstock.com; p. 21 Bettmann/Getty Images; p. 28 DeymosHR/Shutterstock.com; p. 31 Danita Delimont/Gallo Images/Getty Images; p. 35 Institute for Energy Research, EIA, MER, March 2016; p. 36 $250/Moment/Getty Images; p. 39 Ricardo Reitmeyer/Shutterstock.com; p. 58 Ron Eisenbeg/Michael Ochs Archives/Getty Images; p. 62 Julia Waterlow/Corbis/Getty Images; p. 64 Erika J. Mitchell/Shutterstock.com; p. 78 Kevin Dietsch/Pool/Bloomberg/Getty Images; p. 82 Ethan Miller/Getty Images; p. 85 Dake Kang/AP Photo; p. 88 Brian Gordon Green/National Geographic/Getty Images; p. 90 Sander Koning/AFP/Getty Images; p. 92 Tim Robbins/Mint Images/Getty Images.

Printed in the United States of America

TABLE OF CONTENTS

Introduction 5

Chapter 1 11
The History of Alternative Energy

Chapter 2 37
Alternative Energy in the Twenty-First Century

Chapter 3 59
Influence of Alternative Energy on Society

Chapter 4 79
Challenges to the Alternative Energy Movement

Chapter 5 89
The Legacy of the Alternative Energy Movement

Glossary 96

Further Information 99

Bibliography 101

Index 108

About the Author 112

Introduction

To understand the alternative energy movement, it's first important to understand what alternative energy is—and what it's not. Certain types of energy that are formed by natural processes, such as coal, petroleum, and natural gas, are what are known as **fossil fuels**. You might think that fossil fuels are a good thing because they're formed by natural processes, but in reality, fossil fuels present major environmental concerns because they produce great amounts of carbon dioxide. This ultimately contributes to **global warming**. Also, while fossil fuels are formed by natural processes such as the decomposition of materials, it takes millions of years for these processes to unfold and for the fuels to form. This means that as energy sources, they are considered nonrenewable.

Different Energy Sources

In contrast, alternative energy is generally considered to be any energy source that does not use up natural resources or do environmental damage. Most forms of alternative energy are renewable, but not all. Uranium (nuclear power), for instance, is considered an alternative energy source to fossil fuels, and it is nonrenewable. However, while it is true that uranium does not

Opposite: The Google headquarters in Mountain View, California, is topped by an extensive array of solar panels.

This geothermal plant in California converts steam from the earth into electricity.

produce **greenhouse gases** that contribute to **climate change**, it does still create undesirable nuclear waste, so many hesitate to classify it as a true source of alternative energy.

When scientists and manufacturers work on alternative energy solutions designed to decrease humanity's reliance on fossil fuels and limit the pollutants that come from using those fuel sources, they are generally working on solutions involving solar, wind, geothermal, hydro, and biomass energy sources. These solutions involve vehicles that run on alternative fuels, as well as energy solutions that homeowners can implement at their houses and those that business owners can install at the buildings they own or lease.

Promoters of Alternative Energies

The Environmental Protection Agency (EPA), established in 1970 during President Richard Nixon's administration, is the large federal agency involved with many of these efforts, but smaller agencies are key players as well, such as the US Department of Energy's Office of Energy Efficiency and Renewable Energy. State governments also typically have offices dedicated to encouraging the use of renewable energy, such as the California Energy Commission's Renewable Energy Program and the New York State Department of Environmental Conservation.

Major companies such as Apple, Google, Microsoft, Target, and Walmart have also turned a focus onto getting as much power as possible from alternative energy sources, leading the way for smaller businesses to do the same. And of course, the American public has been a driving force in the movement as well, with more and more people looking to alternative energy sources and environmentally friendly products to use in their personal lives.

This hydroelectric dam is in Finland, proving that the United States isn't alone in its interest in using renewable energy sources.

It's an exciting time in the field of alternative energy—and one that is not confined solely to the United States. In fact, the United States actually ranks behind twenty-five other countries in terms of being environmentally friendly, according to a recent study based on data from the 2016 Environmental Performance Index. Finland earned top honors in the list, with its goal of achieving a carbon-neutral society—already, Finland gets nearly two-thirds of its electricity from alternative energy sources. It is closely followed by Iceland, Sweden, and Denmark—two neighboring countries and one country known as a pioneer in its use of geothermal power. A number of other countries in the European Union follow, and the United States comes in twenty-sixth out of more than one hundred countries.

However, as noted, the United States is continually working to improve its use of alternative energy sources and its environmental protections. According to the US Department of Energy, a study done by the National Renewable Energy Laboratory has indicated that the United States will theoretically be able to generate up to 80 percent of its electricity from renewable sources by 2050, primarily through wind and solar power, but also through other renewable energy sources. Whether that will really happen depends on a number of factors, including whether the US government continues to focus significant efforts on developing renewable energy technology. Only time will tell whether the United States will be a world leader in the future development and use of alternative energy sources.

1

The History of Alternative Energy

It might surprise you to realize just how long alternative energy sources have been explored and used and what their beginnings were. Climate change, environmental protections, and alternative fuels are such a talking point in the twenty-first century that they seem to be relatively new topics—but in reality, they aren't at all. Surprisingly, some energy sources that scientists now want to limit the use of actually started out as alternative energy sources!

Wood: The Earliest Consistently Used Energy

The first real energy source commonly used was wood. Wood is obviously a nonrenewable resource—once a tree is cut down, it takes years to grow a new one. Children's author Dr. Seuss famously wrote about the effects of deforestation in *The Lorax* in the early 1970s. The narrator (the Once-ler) recounts how he

Opposite: This reconstruction in Poland shows what hand-operated drilling rigs looked like in the 1800s.

This is an example of a Moorish waterwheel.

cut down the lush Truffula trees to make and sell products, while the Lorax tried to let him know how the environment and the forest creatures would be harmed by his actions:

> I am the Lorax. I speak for the trees.
> I speak for the trees, for the trees have no tongues.
> And I'm asking you, sir, at the top of my lungs—
> he was very upset as he shouted and puffed—
> What's that THING you've made out of my Truffula tuft?

The Lorax repeatedly appeals to the Once-ler to stop cutting down the Truffula forests, but the Once-ler is driven by the money he makes from selling the products he manufactures from the trees. Only when the entire forest has been cut down, the environment polluted, and the forest creatures driven away does the narrator realize that the Lorax was right—and he implores others to take action:

> Now that you're here,
> the word of the Lorax seems perfectly clear.
> Unless someone like you
> cares a whole awful lot,
> nothing is going to get better.
> It's not.

Those words were written in 1971, but the sentiments were known by people as early as the late medieval period (roughly the late fifteenth and early sixteenth centuries), when Europeans recognized the dangers of deforestation and switched to using coal as a fuel source. Although coal is now classified as a fossil fuel, at the time it was an alternative energy.

fact!

In addition to being a nonrenewable energy form, wood was also a pollution-producing energy form. Mummified remains from people who lived in Egypt, Peru, and Great Britain during ancient times show that wood fires burning in homes during that era caused lung damage.

Coal: An Alternative to Deforestation

Coal is a resource millions of years in the making. According to the United States Department of Energy, some three hundred million years ago, when Earth's landmasses were still forming, the climate was warmer and plant-filled swamps and bogs were everywhere. When the trees and plants from these ancient times died, they were eventually buried under mud, rock, and sand, thanks to flooding and other natural environmental changes. They were compacted under hundreds or thousands of feet of earth, sometimes covered by sea, too. In the millions of years that followed, these ancient plants and trees eventually decomposed and turned into fossil fuels. One such fossil fuel was coal, and another was petroleum.

The fossil fuels that were produced depended on the type of material, soil, water, and the temperature while the decomposition was occurring. In the eastern United States, which is still a coal-rich region, the swamps were covered in seawater from the Atlantic Ocean. That seawater contained sulfur, so the coal that was formed was infused with sulfur. This sulfur makes the coal from that region particularly toxic in terms of air pollution when it's burned. The coal found in the western United States burns cleaner because it was not covered in seawater and thus does not have the high sulfur content. No coal burns completely

Coal mines, like this one in West Virginia, used to provide many jobs and a lot of energy. In recent years, however, the focus has turned toward alternative, cleaner energy sources.

The History of Alternative Energy 15

cleanly, but the coal in the eastern United States is particularly pollutant-heavy.

Depending on how long the material has been decomposing and becoming coal, there are different types of coal. Peat is the first stage of coal formation. It was used in earlier times to light fires in homes. Lignite is the second stage, and it is currently used as a fuel for generating electrical power. Lignite also happens to be the first type of coal that is known to have been used. In 4000 BCE, Chinese in the **Neolithic period** used lignite to carve ornaments. During the **Bronze Age**, around the second century BCE, people in what is now Britain were using coal in funeral pyres, which were used in cremation. The Romans were using coal in the region as well, though coal became much more widely used there around 1000 CE. By 1000 BCE, the Chinese were mining coal to burn and use in copper smelting. And Greek scientist Theophrasus wrote about the Greeks' use of coal as a fuel around 200 BCE.

Europeans learned to mine and extract coal from underground around the thirteenth century, when resources near the surface were beginning to be exhausted. When the Industrial Revolution dawned in the late eighteenth century in Britain, coal became an even more widely used resource.

With its increased use, a major drawback of coal as an energy source rapidly became apparent in the form of air pollution. Burning coal releases significant amounts of pollutants into the air. During the Industrial Revolution, the air quality in London was terrible. Smoke from coal burning had already created pollution problems in London, but centralized factories that burned coal during the Industrial Revolution accelerated the problem. In the mid-nineteenth century, the Committee for the Consumption of Smoke at Leeds and the Manchester Association for the Prevention of Smoke were both formed in response to the growing pollution problem, and similar committees were formed in the United States by the end of the nineteenth century.

Governments in Britain, the United States, and Germany began to demand fines from industrial entities that produced too much pollution, but the fines were relatively small, and industries found it in their best interests to continue burning coal to power their factories—coal was so cheap to burn that it made up for the cost of any fines, and besides, there were many exemptions one could use to get around the fines.

Clearly, coal was not a good alternative solution. It is still widely used because it's relatively cheap and easy to use; however, the United States and other countries have been increasingly looking toward energy alternatives that are less harmful to the environment. In 2008, coal provided almost half of the electricity in the United States. By 2012, that number had dropped to approximately 33 percent. According to the US Energy Information Administration, coal consumption in the United States dropped another nearly 5 percent from February 2016 to February 2017.

Whether this decline in coal usage will continue remains to be seen. During his presidential campaign, Donald Trump pledged to bring back jobs in the coal industry that had been lost as the use of coal as an energy source declined in the United States. In the first days and months of his presidency, President Trump followed up on that promise by ending several environmental regulations that had posed challenges for the coal industry.

Petroleum: Development as a Fuel

Before the discovery of electricity and its development into an energy source, people used oil to light lamps. One type of oil commonly used was whale oil, but in the mid 1850s the price for whale oil rose significantly due to a declining whale population. Petroleum was developed as an alternative energy source to whale oil.

Petroleum is a liquid energy source. The most commonly known type of petroleum is **crude oil**, though petroleum can also refer to products that are made from crude oil, such as gas and **kerosene**. Kerosene used to be used to light lamps, though it has since been replaced by electricity in areas where electricity is available. It can also be used as a cooking fuel, and it is currently used as jet and rocket fuel.

Crude oil can be refined and used as an energy source, but it has significant drawbacks. First, petroleum is a fossil fuel and is nonrenewable. Second, oil prices can rise drastically due to a number of factors—for example, much US oil comes from the Middle East, and when political tensions are high with oil-producing countries in the Middle East, it can have an impact on oil prices. Third, oil can damage the environment when oil spills happen and when it is burned for fuel. Burning oil creates air pollution and contributes significantly to global warming.

Like wood, petroleum has been used for centuries—and even millennia! It was plentiful in the Middle East and Asia regions, and history shows it being used as far back as four thousand years ago, in the Babylonian and Persian regions. In Europe, there are records of petroleum being used as far back as the late fifteenth century.

Europeans began refining crude oil by hand in the mid-nineteenth century to create such products as paraffin wax, which is used for electrical insulation. In 1856, Polish pharmacist and inventor Ignacy Lukasiewicz built the first oil refinery. In a refinery, crude oil can be turned into products such as gasoline, diesel fuel, kerosene, and heating oil. Lukasiewicz also invented the first modern street lamp to use kerosene and was instrumental in the construction of the first modern oil well in 1854.

The United States was not far behind Europe in building an oil well—Edwin Drake is reported to have built the first one in the United States in 1859. Drake's well, which was drilled rather than being dug, used a steam engine and kicked off a boom in oil production that really has not ceased. US oil production reached its peak in the 1960s, but Russia, Saudi Arabia, and the United States are still the three major producers of oil worldwide, and approximately 90 percent of fuel for automobiles is derived from oil.

However, petroleum is not a good long-term source of energy, for the reasons mentioned earlier: it is nonrenewable, and using it has a significant impact on the environment. It can also be very expensive, when external factors cause the price of oil to rise. Under President Jimmy Carter, in response to skyrocketing fuel prices, a movement was made in the 1970s to adopt **coal gasification** as an alternative energy source, but that movement fell flat when oil prices ultimately went back down. In terms of environmental impact, the movement would have been a negative one—coal gasification has a significant negative impact on the environment.

Ethanol: Energy from Alcohol

Alexander Graham Bell may be best known for inventing the telephone, but he was also an early proponent of finding renewable energy sources. A 1917 issue of *National Geographic* magazine included a transcript of a commencement address Bell had given, entitled "Prizes for the Inventor: Some of the Problems Awaiting Solution." In it, Bell said:

The Deadly Fog

By the 1950s, scientists were certainly aware that burning coal produced air pollution, but they hadn't yet developed many alternative solutions. Some people underestimated the danger that coal-produced air pollution could actually present. In 1952, that danger became very apparent when thousands of people in London died during a five-day span when the city was blanketed by a dense, dark fog. London's natural environment is often foggy, but in early December 1952, the fog was different—darker, hazier. Visibility was as little as 3 feet (0.9 meters) in some places, making driving impossible. The dark, toxic air was everywhere, and as people tried to walk in the city, they couldn't escape it. It even seeped into their homes through cracks and crevices. London residents suffered from breathing problems that sent more than 150,000 to the hospital, and the toxic fog ultimately claimed an estimated 12,000 lives and also killed thousands of animals.

The cause of this tragedy? According to researchers at Texas A&M University, sulfur dioxide released by burning coal formed sulfuric acid particles in the air that were highly toxic to people. Interestingly, the same issue occurs often in China, which has sixteen of the twenty most-polluted cities in the world. Residents of these Chinese cities often have to wear breathing masks outside during pollution-heavy days.

Like the deadly fog that covered London in 1952, another fog blanketed the city in 1953 (pictured here). This time, citizens were better prepared.

The History of Alternative Energy

20 percent reduction with corn bioethanol), and it reduces carbon dioxide emissions to almost zero.

Like bioethanol, cellulosic ethanol can be incorporated into gasoline and used to power cars, and the EPA tried to increase the amount of cellulosic ethanol that must be incorporated into gas each year from 2010 to 2012. However, the federal court of appeals overruled the EPA in early 2013 and said that the quotas were not realistic, given that production of cellulosic ethanol had started very slowly and thus the supply of the **biofuel** was very limited.

However, several companies have invested millions of dollars into ventures that would ultimately produce commercial-scale cellulosic ethanol production facilities. If those facilities are indeed developed, there is potential for cellulosic ethanol to become a major viable source for alternative energy in the future.

Water: A Potential Powerhouse

People have long known that water can be used as a power source. Waterwheels can convert the energy of falling water into power and were used for this purpose by people in the Greek and Mediterranean regions as early as the **Hellenistic period**, between 300 and roughly 30 BCE. The ancient Egyptians had used a primitive form of the waterwheel even earlier, around 400 BCE.

Use of the waterwheel in various forms continued throughout Europe and Asia over the following centuries, and waterpower was widely used during the Industrial Revolution, declining only when coal became more heavily used as an energy source.

In the late nineteenth century, waterpower was combined with electricity generation, and hydroelectric power became a new

Brazil: A Leader in Bioethanol Use

Brazil has emerged as a leader in a particular sector of the alternative energy field for their use of ethanol as a fuel. They primarily use Brazilian sugarcane to produce ethanol, which is superior to the United States method of using corn to produce ethanol because producing ethanol from sugar requires less energy than producing it from corn.

Brazil has actually long been at the front of the bioethanol field. In 1976, their government put in place requirements to blend gas with ethanol, and in 1978, the country produced the first car to run entirely on ethanol. The United States actually produces more than twice as much ethanol as Brazil, but Brazil uses more ethanol in their automobile fuel than the United States does—25 percent compared to the United States' 10 percent.

technology in England in 1878. The United States was actually slightly ahead of England in this pursuit, as they recognized a major potential source of hydroelectric power right in their backyard: Niagara Falls. The Niagara Falls Hydraulic Power and Manufacturing Company powerhouse opened in 1874, though its energy production was minimal. However, Jacob F. Schoellkopf purchased and improved the powerhouse and the canal that led to it, and opened the Schoellkopf Power Station No. 1 in 1881, which ended up being a significant source of hydroelectric power. Schoellkopf went on to open other powerhouses powered by Niagara Falls as well.

By 1889, the United States had two hundred operating hydroelectric power stations, and the development further continued with the building of the Hoover Dam, the Bonneville Dam, and the Grand Coulee Dam (the largest hydropower plant in the United States and the second largest in the world). As of 2017, the United States had more than two thousand hydroelectric power stations, which provided about 49 percent of the nation's renewable electricity.

Like virtually all energy sources, the use of hydroelectric power isn't without its drawbacks. Building hydroelectric plants is expensive. Also, the amount of energy produced directly correlates to the amount of available water—during times of drought, there is obviously less water available to produce power. There are environmental concerns, too. Some forms of hydroelectric power require damming, which changes the region's natural waterflow and can affect fish, other animals in the region, and plant life.

Wind: Harnessing Energy from the Air

Like power from water, power from wind has long been used. The sails used on early rafts and boats took advantage of wind power—sailors used sails to capture the wind that could propel them across lakes and seas. Also, people have used wind power for more than two thousand years to grind grain and pump water.

Britain, a leader of energy developments during the Industrial Revolution, was the site of the first windmill used to generate electrical power. In Scotland in 1887, a university professor built a windmill to capture the wind and use that power to charge energy storage devices called accumulators that could in turn provide lighting in his house. That same professor later built a wind turbine to provide emergency power to a local asylum.

Around the same time, an American named Charles Brush invented a similar—but larger—turbine to harness wind power at his home. His turbine reportedly could power up to one hundred lightbulbs, several lamps, and some motors in his laboratory. He also used the wind power to charge a bank of batteries.

Later, wind farms were created, particularly in the United States, China, and Germany. These farms are essentially large groups of wind turbines clustered in one location—either on land or in the ocean. For land-based wind farms, which may be as big as several hundred square miles, the land in between the turbines can be used for agricultural purposes, such as livestock grazing.

> *fact!*
>
> There are five power stations on the Niagara River. Niagara Falls spans the international border with Canada, thus two power plants are in the United States, and three are in Canada. Despite the United States having fewer power plants than Canada, the production capacity of the two US power plants is actually greater.

Niagara Falls is both beautiful and useful, providing an excellent source of hydroelectric power.

The United States pioneered the use of wind farms. A small five-turbine "farm" was built in North Dakota in 1940, but it was not considered a full-fledged wind farm by today's standards. Therefore, the first official wind farm was a twenty-turbine farm in New Hampshire, built in 1980. Since then, the use of wind power has grown quickly in the United States. In 2016, wind power accounted for 5.55 percent of all generated electrical energy in the United States, according to the US Department of Energy.

Like other energy sources, wind power has drawbacks. For one, it's expensive to set up a wind farm. Wind farms also may not be cost effective in less windy parts of the United States. On a similar note, windy locations with room for wind farm development tend to be located far from cities, where the electricity generated would ultimately be used. That means electrical lines would need to be built from the remote location to the city where the power could be used. This would be expensive and not particularly aesthetically pleasing!

Some also cite the ugly appearance of wind farms as a drawback. The large turbines obviously alter the landscape. And they do create a noise disturbance. Similarly, the turbines can be dangerous to local wildlife—namely, birds and bats that are killed when they fly into the turbines.

Sun: Our Brightest Power Source

Solar energy is another alternative form, using the light and heat from the sun as power. Solar energy can be used for heating (such as swimming pools) and energy (via **photovoltaics** and solar thermal energy).

Like many other forms of alternative energy, solar energy has been used for millennia. In the seventh century BCE, humans began to concentrate sunlight through magnifying glasses to start fires. Greek inventor Archimedes reportedly used mirrors to reflect concentrated sunlight onto enemy ships, which would cause them to catch fire. In 1767, Swiss physicist Horace Benedict de Saussure created the first solar oven—something schoolchildren still build today when learning about solar power! In 1839, French physicist Edmund Becquerel discovered photovoltaics when he recognized that material exposed to light can create voltage. Nearly fifty years later, American inventor Charles Fritts came up with early designs for creating solar cells to harness solar power, though the first solar cell wasn't officially created until 1954, when three scientists from Bell Labs created a photovoltaic cell that could convert sunlight into electrical power and patented their design.

In the early twentieth century, a US inventor and engineer named Frank Shuman was experimenting with solar thermal energy, creating a solar engine system that he patented in 1912. That same year, he built the first solar thermal power station in the world, located in Egypt. A series of events including the outbreak of World War I and the increasing use of petroleum meant that Shuman's technology wasn't widely adopted, but the ideas behind it were revisited in the 1970s, when solar energy became an area of interest again.

According to the Institute for Energy Research, solar energy accounts for only 0.5 percent of the energy consumed in the United States, which makes it the least used of the renewable energy sources. One might wonder why that's the case. The sun is a constant in our environment, even when it's hidden behind clouds. The reality, though, is that it's *not* that constant. It's constant in that it's always there, but its power is greatly affected by changes in the atmosphere, such as clouds and dust. Also, the solar energy that reaches Earth's atmosphere is relatively weak—the atmosphere filters the power of the sun pretty significantly, otherwise Earth and its inhabitants would be scorched by the sun's power.

Similarly, it's fairly easy for one family to install solar panels on their roof to capture solar energy and use that in their home, but actually powering an entire city is a whole different story. Doing so would require miles and miles of space for huge photovoltaic installations to be placed. The Institute for Energy Research estimates that to meet the electricity needs of the United States, they would need an area of about 10,000 square miles (25,899 square kilometers) for the solar panels—that's the size of Rhode Island and New Hampshire combined!

Here are some of the wind turbines in Hawaii. If fully harnessed, the wind there has enough power to provide electricity to the entire state.

Further, some areas of the country are sunnier than others. The Southwest, for example, gets a lot of sun, but how could the solar energy be transmitted to other, less sunny places? It would require large, unsightly transmission lines—and ugliness aside, those transmission lines tend to degrade the power as it passes through them.

The drawbacks to solar energy are in many ways similar to those of wind energy—for example, lack of space and changes to the landscape. Like wind energy, solar energy is not inexpensive to set up. Although solar energy shows promise for the future, these drawbacks have slowed its growth as an alternative energy source.

Geothermal: Energy from the Earth

Another type of alternative energy is geothermal. The prefix *geo* means "earth," and *thermal* means "hot"—and that's exactly what geothermal energy is: heat from the earth. Specifically, it is energy that is generated from radioactive decay and from when the planet was originally formed.

Geothermal energy has been used for as long as humans have been on the planet. Humans used hot springs, which are naturally occurring, to bathe during the **Paleolithic period**, and the ancient Romans used geothermal energy for heating enclosed areas. Native Americans living in an area of California called The Geysers have used steam and hot water for cooking and for healing purposes for thousands of years—which makes sense, given that The Geysers is the largest geothermal field in the world. The French have operated a geothermal district heating system in Chaudes-Aigues, a spa town in central France, since the fourteenth century. The first known industrial use of geothermal energy occurred in 1827, when the power from geyser steam was used to extract boric acid from volcanic mud in Larderello, Italy. In that same general region, the Italians built the first commercial geothermal power plant in 1911.

In 1892, the United States created its first district heating system in Boise, Idaho, followed shortly thereafter by one in Klamath Falls, Oregon. A few years later, in Union County, Oregon, construction was finished on the first building (a hotel) to use geothermal energy for its primary source of heat. In the 1920s, geothermal wells and geysers were used to heat greenhouses in Boise, Idaho; Iceland; and Tuscany, Italy. Iceland is home to many geysers, and Icelanders in the 1940s began using the geothermal energy released by them to heat their homes. Also in the 1940s, geothermal heat pumps were first successfully used to draw heat from the ground.

In 1960, Pacific Gas and Electric (PG&E) opened the first geothermal electrical power plant in the United States—perhaps not surprisingly, at The Geysers in California. The region currently contains twenty-two geothermal power plants that draw steam from hundreds of wells.

The United States is currently the second biggest user of geothermal power in the world, running only slightly behind China as of 2015. The United States uses more than five times as much geothermal energy as the next country in the list, Turkey. The United States also produces more geothermal electricity than any other country, with the Philippines coming in a distant second.

There are many positives to using geothermal energy. Among them is the fact that geothermal energy is renewable and does not cause significant pollution. However, there are some drawbacks, too. In theory, building geothermal power plants can cause earthquakes—construction of one such plant caused a magnitude 3.4 earthquake in Switzerland in 1997. Also, cost is an issue—building the plants is expensive, as is building the heating/cooling systems that use the energy. Location is the third drawback: geothermal energy can be extracted in very specific areas, usually where **tectonic plates** meet. Iceland, the Philippines, and a region in Northern California are all rich with geothermal resources, but there are many other areas that aren't. The energy can be transported to other areas, but greater energy loss occurs the farther it travels.

In short, the history of energy usage—and alternative energy forms specifically—is much longer than one might immediately think. All of these energy resources have advantages as well as drawbacks—there is no single perfect solution. However, as we have entered the twenty-first century, with climate change and environmental protections at the forefront of many people's minds, scientists continue to look for ways to harness and use alternative energy sources without causing environmental harm.

US Energy Consumption in 2016

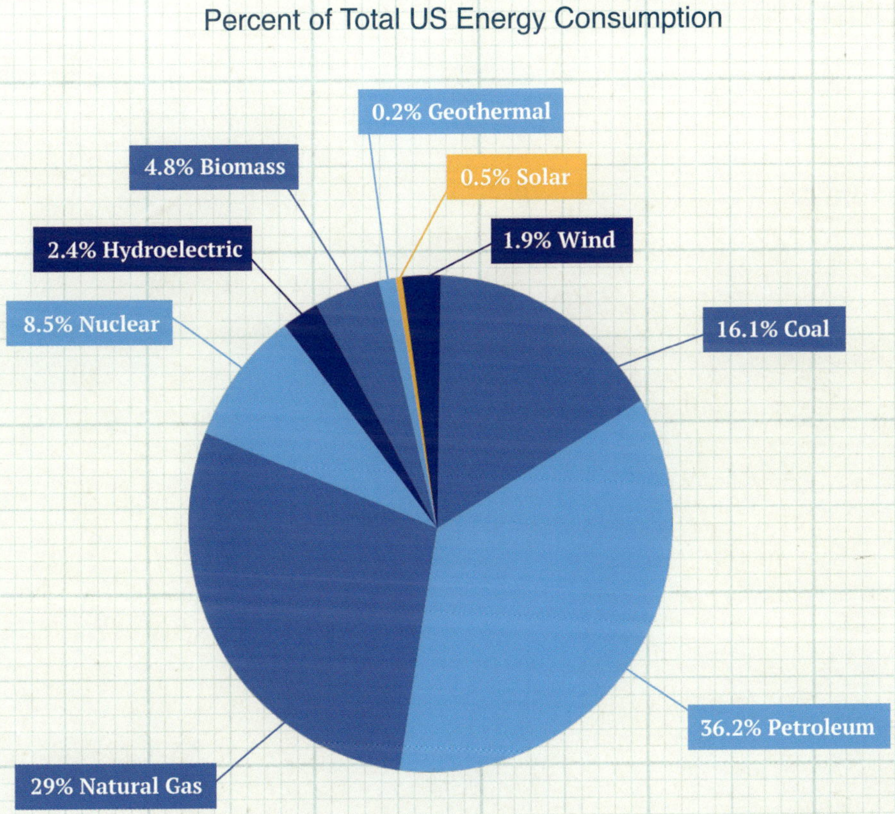

Percent of Total US Energy Consumption

- 0.2% Geothermal
- 0.5% Solar
- 1.9% Wind
- 4.8% Biomass
- 2.4% Hydroelectric
- 8.5% Nuclear
- 16.1% Coal
- 29% Natural Gas
- 36.2% Petroleum

The History of Alternative Energy

2

Alternative Energy in the Twenty-First Century

The twenty-first century has been a time of extensive growth in the field of alternative energy sources. In the United States and several other countries, increased awareness of the eventual scarcity of fossil fuels has prompted much research and development in alternative energy sources. At the close of the twentieth century, the International Energy Agency commented that "the world is in the early stages of an inevitable transition to a sustainable energy system that will be largely dependent on renewable resources." As the world moved into the new millennium, it was clear that attention needed to be paid to alternative energy sources.

Wind and solar power received particular attention during the early years of the twenty-first century. In 2004, the Worldwatch Institute, an independent research organization that works on environmental sustainability, among other social issues, reported

Opposite: This large biomass facility is located in Indian River County, Florida.

that wind and solar energy sources had expanded at double-digit rates for the previous decade. However, that expansion was mostly in six countries: the United States, Denmark, Germany, India, Japan, and Spain. It's no coincidence that these six countries have governments that made conscious decisions to promote and encourage use of alternative energy.

To understand where alternative energy has been developing in recent years and to get a glimpse of where it may continue to develop as the twenty-first century continues, it's useful to consider a timeline of roughly the last two decades and what growth has been made in the alternative energy field.

Solar Energy

Solar energy may be the best-known, most commonplace form of alternative energy. Solar-powered calculators have existed for many years. People have been using solar panels to heat swimming pools for decades. More and more, people are using solar panels on their houses to heat their homes, too. An increasing number of businesses and corporations are also installing solar panels on buildings to provide an alternative energy source.

Between 1994 and 2004, solar energy capacity grew 22 percent. Energy produced by photovoltaics grew sharply in the first few years of the twenty-first century. The world produced its first gigawatt of photovoltaic capacity in 1999, but in the next four years it tripled that number, with photovoltaic production above 3 gigawatts.

Much development for harnessing solar energy took place from the mid-twentieth century and beyond. The key to harnessing solar energy was in developing solar cells that had photoelectric properties and could efficiently capture the sun's

The same sun that helps crops like wheat to grow can be a source of alternative energy.

energy. A major step forward happened in 1954, when Bell Labs debuted the first high-power silicon photovoltaic cell. Silicon is still widely used in photovoltaics, accounting for the majority of solar cells on the market. However, silicon technologies have expanded widely over the years, and now there are numerous types used in the production of solar cells, roughly categorized into two main types: crystalline silicon and thin-film technology.

Technically, photovoltaic cells can be made out of other types of **semiconductor** materials as well. They don't even necessarily have to use just one material. Single-junction solar cells use a single layer of semiconductor material, but multi-junction cells use multiple configurations and semiconductor materials to more effectively absorb light.

Perhaps not surprisingly, single-junction versus multi-junction cells provide different efficiencies with regard to light absorption. In theory, the maximum efficiency of a single-junction cell is just over 33 percent absorption, while a multi-junction cell could absorb up to nearly 87 percent of highly concentrated sunlight. These are theoretical numbers, though. In lab situations, single-junction cells have generally shown to be 20 to 25 percent efficient, whereas multi-junction cells have shown to be just over 46 percent efficient. Still, it's obvious from both sets of numbers that multi-junction cells are more efficient in their absorption of solar energy.

So why not always use multi-junction solar cells and make the most of the sun's energy? A simple reason: cost. The cost of building and using multi-junction solar cells is too high to be practical for most applications. If the cost is higher than the amount of money that would be saved by using the technology, then it's really not practical. Multi-junction solar cells have been used in some very specialized applications, though, such as Mars rover missions.

It's likely that as solar technology continues to develop, costs will decrease, and multi-junction solar cells may become more widely used. Certainly, there are exciting developments happening in solar-energy research that are making it an increasingly more viable source of alternative energy.

For example, scientists at such institutions as the National Renewable Energy Laboratory have been further developing perovskite solar cells. Perovskite is a mineral found in Earth's **mantle**, and it can work as the semiconductor material in photovoltaic cells. In a matter of five years, between 2009 and 2014, scientific research took its efficiency as a solar technology from less than 5 percent to more than 20 percent. Scientists recently discovered that using both perovskite and kesterite (another mineral) improves power conversion in solar cells, too. Perovskite solar cells are also relatively inexpensive to produce, which makes them a promising new technology for the solar energy field.

Another relatively inexpensive solar technology that is gaining attention is the use of dye-sensitized solar cells, also called DSSCs. The efficiency of DSSCs isn't quite as good as that of traditional thin-film single-junction solar cells, but their cost is low enough to make DSSCs a very worthwhile technology for large-scale solar energy use.

Similarly, organic solar cells and **polymer** solar cells are inexpensive to produce and thus could potentially be used on large-scale projects. However, as of the time of this writing their energy conversion efficiency is relatively low, at just over 10 percent efficiency.

In addition to wind power, Hawaii uses solar panels to harness solar energy.

Thin-film solar cells are relatively inexpensive, as photovoltaics go, but their light absorption efficiency is lowered because of their thinness. One possible solution scientists are investigating is using surface texturing. Basically, a flat surface tends to reflect a lot of light rays, and on a textured surface, much of the light is bounced back onto the cell instead. This increases light absorption and thus also increases efficiency. In 2012, researchers at MIT revealed that using inverted pyramids as a form of surface texturing, they could increase light absorption to equal that of a material thirty times thicker than the typical thin-cell solar film.

Current research is also looking at ways to improve **photon** up conversion and down conversion. In up conversion, two low-energy photons are combined to form one photon with greater energy. In down conversion, the reverse is true: one higher-energy photon can be broken into two lower-energy photons. Both up conversion and down conversion can make solar cells more efficiently use the photons harnessed from the sun.

One issue with solar energy is that sunlight isn't constant. Scientists are working to address this challenge by investigating technologies such as adaptive cells. These solar cells can both absorb and reflect light, and they change, which they do based on the environmental conditions. When light is intense, the surface of the cell becomes adaptive (or absorbent). This allows the intense light to penetrate the cell. Meanwhile, the rest of the cell is reflective. This helps to increase the amount of absorbed light that is retained in the cell.

In 2014, Glint Photonics introduced an adaptive material for solar cells that would automatically switch the cell's surface from reflective to adaptive as intense light moved across it. That technology has existed in manual form for a while. Scientists have known that they could use lenses and mirrors to focus intense sunlight on small portions of cells for better absorption. But this was a difficult process, and Glint Photonics' adaptive material addressed this challenge and, according to Glint's CEO, could result in solar power dropping from 8 cents per kilowatt hour (the cost using the current best conventional solar panels) to 4 cents per kilowatt hour (the cost using Glint's cells).

Regardless of the specific solar-cell technology used, the ultimate process is much the same. Solar photovoltaic devices absorb sunlight and convert it directly into electricity. This is why a solar-powered calculator works instantly—the tiny solar cell inside it can automatically convert light into energy used to power the calculator.

Solar energy naturally requires sunlight, which means photovoltaics need to be installed in areas that typically get a lot of sun. A solar farm in, say, Seattle, Washington, wouldn't be terribly useful, given that the region tends to be overcast much of the year!

In theory, if scientists covered 4 percent of the world's deserts with photovoltaic cells, they could collect enough solar energy to fulfill all of the world's daily electricity needs. However, storing and transferring that energy is an issue. Desert areas tend not to be heavily populated, so the energy would need to be transferred to populated areas. There is energy loss inherent in transferring it, not to mention the fact that electrical lines are unsightly and relatively expensive to maintain. If solar energy is to become the dominant form of energy used, scientists need to figure out a solution to these challenges, while also increasing absorption and efficiency and bringing down costs.

Wind Energy

While solar energy is used all over the United States on homes and buildings, wind energy tends to be a bit more localized. It's used in areas that tend to have a lot of wind *and* have the land space to install wind farms. Nevertheless, wind power has experienced extremely high growth in the twenty-first century. Between 1994 and 2004, wind energy capacity grew an astounding 30 percent—faster even than solar energy. When those numbers were calculated in 2004, it was estimated that worldwide wind capacity could power the equivalent of nineteen million households!

Perhaps this growth is at least partially attributable to cost. A 2004 report from the Worldwatch Institute estimated the cost of wind power at 3.1 to 5.3 cents per kilowatt hour. For comparison, that same report showed the cost of coal-driven power at 6.6 to 21.7 cents per kilowatt hour. The most expensive was solar power, estimated at 24.7 to 48.7 cents per kilowatt hour.

The cost of wind power has dropped even further since the Worldwatch Institute's report. In 2017, the US Department of Energy estimated that wind power cost an average of just 2.35 cents per kilowatt hour in the United States. In 1980, the cost of wind-generated power was approximately 55 cents per kilowatt hour, so the drop to 2.35 cents per kilowatt hour in just over thirty-five years is nothing short of astounding. Wind power is clearly inexpensive and renewable—assuming a country has the space and ability to set up a wind farm.

Obviously, wind is required to harness energy from wind power. However, in the early twenty-first century, advances were made to decrease the amount of wind required for a successful wind farm. At the Sandia National Laboratory, the US Department of Energy developed wind turbines that featured lighter, larger blades that rotated more slowly, which were capable of harnessing wind power at less windy sites. These turbines and blades expanded wind development potential by an impressive 12 percent. The Department of Energy estimated as of 2017 that the average capacity factor, which is used to measure power plant productivity, was 33 percent, an increase of 3 percent over the average capacity factor in 2000 and an increase of 11 percent over the average capacity factor in 1980.

The Department of Energy has a division called the Wind Program, which partners with scientists and equipment manufacturers to work on projects that increase performance and reliability of wind technology while lowering costs. The Wind Program has worked extensively on refining wind turbines for increased reliability, productivity, and cost effectiveness. Not only do today's turbines gather more energy, but they have also become quite a lucrative business source. According to the Wind Program, wind turbine technology exports were $488 million in

2014, up from $16 million in 2007—more than thirty times the total export value in just seven years.

The Wind Program worked with industry giant General Electric over a course of twenty years to refine wind energy components. One result is the GE Wind Energy 1.5 megawatt (MW) wind turbine, which makes up nearly half of the turbines used in wind farms in the United States and is also used globally. The Wind Program also partnered with Siemens Energy and the National Renewable Energy Laboratory in Boulder, Colorado, in the development of a 2.3 MW wind turbine.

Engineers are also looking at building higher wind towers. Using technology for wind mapping, scientists have discovered that wind speeds are consistently higher at higher levels above the ground, so engineers are experimenting with different tower materials and heights, as well as blade sizes, to capture greater wind power at higher levels of air. According to the vice president of Leeco Steel, "Steel is regarded as one of the most flexible materials in structural engineering, and we believe that holds true for the latest designs in taller towers for the wind industry … New designs of base sections with thicker-walled steel of higher grades of steel allows wind turbine OEMs [original equipment manufacturers] to reach new heights while staying true to their proven tower designs of today and the past twenty years."

Globally, Germany and Denmark developed mathematical climate models to help scientists predict wind resources twenty-four to thirty-six hours in advance. This development allows wind farms to prepare for and effectively manage wind power. Scientists also developed variable speed operation for wind turbines, which further allowed them to best harness the energy potential from the wind at any given time.

Office of Energy Efficiency and Renewable Energy

The US Department of Energy has an office called the Office of Energy Efficiency and Renewable Energy (EERE) that hopes to help propel the United States in the movement to a global clean energy economy. Among other goals, EERE hopes to increase the generation of electrical power from hydropower, solar, wind, wave, tidal, and geothermal power. The EERE maintains offices specifically for research and development in the areas of geothermal, solar, wind, and water power.

Advances in technology have also allowed for the development of both onshore and offshore wind farms. Onshore wind farms are obviously easier to manage—they tend to be more easily accessible than a wind farm located out in the ocean! But offshore wind farms have benefits as well. The wind offshore is typically more consistent and stronger. Stronger winds means more energy to harness, and the consistency is key in reducing the wear and tear on the turbines and other equipment. Off the coast of Rhode Island, the Block Island Wind Farm has a 30 MW capacity, for example.

One development taking place in offshore wind farms is research into floating wind turbines. The offshore turbines have traditionally been built on permanent underwater foundations, but floating wind towers would be easier and less expensive to install.

Hydropower

While much research is taking place in the fields of solar and wind energy, those two forms actually only make up 0.5 percent and 1.9 percent, respectively, of the total energy consumption in the United States, according to the Institute for Energy Research in 2016. Hydroelectric energy, on the other hand, accounts for 2.4 percent of US energy consumption—as much as wind and solar energy combined! In fact, over the last decade in the United States, the Office of Energy Efficiency and Renewable Energy reports that hydroelectric power has provided more than 6 percent of the United States' total electricity.

Worldwide, hydroelectric power made up more than 16 percent of the world's total electricity in 2015, and that number was expected to increase by more than 3 percent per year for the next twenty-five years. As such, there has been extensive research and developments in the field.

A couple of factors make hydroelectricity very attractive as an alternative energy source. For one, producing hydroelectricity is relatively inexpensive compared to some other alternative energy technologies. The average cost of electricity from a large hydro station is between 3 and 5 cents per kilowatt hour. Although prices for solar energy range greatly, in general it is more than 5 cents per kilowatt hour—sometimes significantly more. Hydroelectricity is also a very renewable energy source because it does not consume any water. The water doesn't have to be consumed for its power to be used—it is simply the force of the water's movement that is used for energy.

Because of the promise of hydropower as an alternative energy source, the US Department of Energy has developed the Water Power Program, which helps to develop and deploy new technologies to enhance hydropower generation. One technology the Water Power Program is investing in is low-head hydropower technology. Originally, hydropower facilities tended to be developed at places like Niagara Falls, where there was a significant change in elevation that resulted in fast-moving water and thus the potential for significant energy capture. Low-head hydropower technology allows scientists to capture hydropower at water sites that have a much-lesser change in elevation, such as canals, water conduits, and non-powered dams.

One example of low-head hydropower technology is the Archimedean screw hydro turbine. In ancient times, these screw pumps were used to draw water *upward* to a higher level, for irrigation purposes—water could be taken from a water source and brought to irrigate crops at a higher elevation. In hydropower, the screw is essentially used in reverse: water from a slightly higher *fact!*

According to the Energy Information Administration's data from 2015, China produces the most hydroelectricity worldwide. Canada is second, followed by Brazil. The United States is the fourth-largest producer of hydroelectricity worldwide.

elevation flows into the screw, and the pressure of the water flowing downward through the screw causes the screw to rotate, generating power that is pulled out by an electrical generator connected to the screw shaft.

The Water Power Program also works on optimizing water use at hydropower facilities and on investigating new materials that can improve performance and lower operating costs of hydropower facilities. For example, materials that can increase the lifespan of hydropower equipment can help lower overall costs. As hydropower facilities age, so does the equipment at them, and the Water Power Program works to track data on equipment deterioration and research new materials and technologies that will keep equipment functioning efficiently for a longer time. One such project the Water Power Program supported involved Natel Energy and Alden Research Laboratory, who built a reliable powertrain for a hydropower turbine called the hydroEngine. The hydroEngine works with low-head hydropower technology and resulted in energy cost savings of about $2 per megawatt hour.

Efficiency is also increased when facilities are kept updated, and the Water Power Program works on projects like this as well. Three projects the Water Power Program worked on in New

Mexico, Colorado, and Washington resulted in an increase of more than 3,000 megawatt-hours per year.

Further, the Water Power Program works on projects that will not only optimize power output but will also minimize environmental impact. Together with a number of national laboratories, the Water Power Program developed the Water-Use Optimization Toolset (WUOT), which helps hydropower plants run as efficiently as possible, with as minimal an environmental impact as possible. The tools included in WUOT help engineers work with hydrologic forecasting, day-ahead scheduling, environmental performance, and real-time operation. In other words, they can use these tools to consider environmental factors and maximize plant performance while minimizing environmental impact.

The Water Power Program is a well-known entity in the world of hydropower, given their affiliation with the Department of Energy. However, they are not the only entity doing research and development into hydropower programs. Far from it, actually! Verdant Power is one company working in the field of hydropower, marine, and **hydrokinetic** technologies. They are behind a number of renewable energy projects, one of which involved putting wind turbines into the East River in New York City. This project was approved in 2012 and was in progress as of 2017.

Another technology that many scientists have investigated is harnessing the hydrokinetic energy generated by ocean waves. The Pacific Coast holds particular promise for this because of the sheer power of the waves, both onshore and offshore. The West Coast of the United States is known for its rocky beaches and powerful waves that are terrific for surfing but dangerous for swimming. Unlike the calmer waters at East Coast and Gulf Coast beaches, the power of the waves on the West Coast is immense.

At the seventh European Wave and Tidal Energy Conference held in 2007, scientists estimated that if a mere 15 percent of energy available in US coastal waves was extracted, it would generate as much electricity as is currently produced at conventional hydroelectric dams. They further stated that the amount of energy that could be captured from US waves, tides, and river currents could power more than sixty-seven million typical US households.

In 2012, Ocean Renewable Power Company developed one of the first tidal power projects in the United States to deliver power to the **electrical grid**. The underwater turbine harnesses enough energy as the tide rushes into and out of a bay off the coast of Maine to power twenty-five to thirty homes.

The current of a river is generally not as powerful as the current of the ocean, but that doesn't mean it's a useless energy source. Scientists have found ways to harness power in rivers, too. Dams are one way, but they can be eyesores and can negatively impact the environment. A California-based energy company found a way to harness river power without damming by instead installing modules made up of a turbine, a stabilizer, a mooring system, and an energy conversion periodically across a river. As the water flows through these modules, the turbines spin and drive a generator. Their scientists found that this module system could generate up to 50 kilowatts of energy from a river with a water speed of only 4 **knots**.

Another method for harnessing energy from a river was developed in 2007, when University of Michigan professor Michael Bernitsas studied how fish move through a river. Based on what he saw, he developed a device called VIVACE, which stands for Vortex Induced Vibration for Aquatic Clean Energy. VIVACE is now licensed to Vortex Hydro Energy. The device uses a series of cylinders placed on the bottom of a water source. The current flows over the cylinders and creates **vortices**, much like fish create vortices by curving their bodies as they swim through the water. The artificially created vortices move the cylinders up and down and, in doing so, generate an electrical current. VIVACE shows a great deal of promise as a hydropower technology because it can be used effectively even in slow-moving bodies of water.

Another promising technology is the use of pipe power. Water pipes exist throughout cities—sewer lines, wastewater pipes, and various water conduits. An Israeli–US company called Leviathan Energy decided to use the energy being wasted as liquid rushed through those pipes. They invented a water turbine that can be enclosed in municipal pipes to generate electricity as water or other liquids rush through the pipes. Imagine that: creating energy just by flushing your toilet!

Innovations in the hydropower field are happening rapidly, making hydroelectric power a very viable source of alternative energy in the future.

Geothermal Energy

Although the United States is the second-largest consumer of geothermal energy worldwide (behind only China), geothermal energy still does not make up a significant part of the total US energy consumption, at only 0.2 percent. That's partly due to the cost of building and maintaining geothermal power plants, but also due to the potential environmental impacts and difficult conditions that come with drilling into the earth to harness geothermal power.

Research and development are under way to address these challenges and make geothermal energy a more viable

fact!

Both photovoltaics and solar thermal panels absorb solar energy for use by humans. However, photovoltaics use that solar energy to create electricity, whereas solar thermal systems are used specifically for heating.

energy solution, though. The US Department of Energy cited the work of Baker Hughes Incorporated, an oilfield services company, in developing an advanced drilling system that could handle the extreme temperatures and pressures as well as the crystalline rock formations that come when drilling deep into the earth. In 2017, Baker Hughes demonstrated that their drilling system could drill at extremely high temperatures (around 572 degrees Fahrenheit, or 300 degrees Celsius) for an astounding 270 hours, which is the longest time such a system has ever operated. The Department of Energy claimed Baker Hughes's technology might have far-reaching impacts for geothermal energy, as well as for fossil and nuclear energy sectors. However, this technology is not without some environmental concern. The Department of Energy has suggested that Baker Hughes's system could help engineers tap into enhanced geothermal systems (EGSs), which are essentially man-made geothermal reservoirs created when engineers inject fluid into the earth to cause it to crack along preexisting fractures, giving them access to the hot rock beneath the surface. In other words, the energy exists below the surface of the earth, but it's trapped because there are no fractures for the energy to be released through. So engineers manufacture fractures along preexisting lines. This is not unlike the controversial process of **fracking**, which is used for extracting gas and oil. The Department of Energy estimates that expanding EGSs could lead to harnessing enough geothermal energy to power more than one hundred million US homes. Certainly that is impressive, but it remains to be seen whether this new technology will be widely implemented, given the possible environmental impacts.

On a smaller scale, though, geothermal energy is becoming increasingly more used. Small geothermal pumps can be installed to power homes, requiring only a 3-foot-wide (0.9-meter-wide) area of earth to bore into for the pump installation. In other words, even homes with very small backyards can be candidates for a geothermal pump and energy system.

Some schools and commercial buildings have also opted to install geothermal pumps to supply energy to their buildings. By 2013, more than 250 schools in Texas had contracted with Image Engineering to install geothermal heat pumps, and other firms had done similar installations at schools in Pennsylvania, New Jersey, and New York.

Developments in geothermal pump technology have also helped speed their adoption. The pumps originally were hardwired to their control devices, which meant that problems could crop up with the wiring, requiring a service call. But now most pumps use wireless technology for their controllers, which allows for real-time monitoring of the pump's operation and efficiency, and eliminates problems with hardwiring.

Biomass Energy

Biomass energy, such as that produced by ethanol, accounts for 4.8 percent of the total US energy consumption, according to the Institute for Energy Research. It's a renewable resource because the biomass materials (plant materials and animal waste, generally) can regenerate relatively quickly. However, there are some environmental concerns with using biomass. For instance, the biomass materials are often burned to release their energy, which can contribute to air pollution and global warming. Growing plant materials for biomass can also use a lot of water (a resource that is in short supply in many parts of the world), and, if overharvested, biomass materials can impact the environmental balance of the ecosystem.

Nevertheless, if these risks can be managed, biomass offers potential as an alternative energy source, so research into it continues. A European alternative energy company, Vattenfall, is looking at a thermal processing technique that would produce a biomass pellet that has a higher energy value—in other words, more energy potential in a smaller package.

Worldwide, scientists are studying how cofiring biomass, which is carbon-neutral, along with coal, which is carbon-producing, can limit the environmental impact of burning the materials. Engineers are also looking at ways to use municipal solid waste (a.k.a. garbage) as biomass. A proposed power plant that would burn solid waste would use a system that would remove pollutants from gas produced by burning the waste, thus limiting the potential environmental impact.

Tripling Alternative Energy Efforts

A fascinating development in geothermal technology occurred in Nevada in late 2015. California leads the United States in geothermal capacity, but Nevada is second. At the Stillwater Geothermal Power Plant near Fallon, Nevada, Enel Green Power established the first ever hybrid solar-geothermal project. This facility is actually considered the world's first triple-hybrid power facility because it combines geothermal power with both photovoltaics and solar thermal power generation. The plant has a capacity of 61 megawatts of power generation: 33 MW of geothermal power, 26 MW of solar photovoltaics, and 2 MW of solar thermal power.

3

Influence of Alternative Energy on Society

Alternative energy has been a huge talking point in the United States in the twenty-first century, influencing everything from personal choices to political campaigns. The United States became increasingly aware of environmental pollution in the late 1960s and early 1970s. The air hovering over major cities was heavy with smog, particularly in places like Los Angeles, where mountains created a sort of "bowl" in which the polluted air would sit, day after day. The booming population in Los Angeles didn't help, either—more people meant more cars, which meant more pollution.

This awareness around pollution led to the signing of the Clean Air Act in 1970 and the formation of the Environmental Protection Agency. Since then, Americans have continued to pay attention to environmental pollutants. While Los Angeles and other large cities are no longer choked with the dangerous

Opposite: In the 1970s, the smog in Los Angeles, California, could be so thick that it was nearly impossible to see skyscrapers.

smog of the late 1960s and early 1970s, air pollution does still exist, and US scientists and agencies are continually researching alternative forms of energy that will reduce pollution, as well as preserving natural resources that will be threatened if the use of fossil fuels continues unchecked.

Personal Responses to the Alternative Energy Movement

While it might be easy to dismiss the impact a single person can have on the environment, it shouldn't be. Every person who works to incorporate alternative energy sources into their life contributes to preserving the planet's resources. And there is strength in numbers, so the fact that the alternative energy movement has influenced many, many people in the United States means that collectively, individuals are making a big difference.

Using Alternative Energy in Homes

In the past, homes were generally heated with gas furnaces or propane—or, looking further back, with wood-burning stoves and fireplaces. Most homes built nowadays still have a gas furnace or propane, but many homeowners are now choosing to install solar panels on their roofs (or in some cases, in their yards), and some home builders are automatically installing them when they build new home communities.

Solar panels used on residential homes typically generate about 10 watts per square foot, and generally a few square feet of panels on the roof will be enough to power the home. An even newer innovation is solar shingles, which actually take the place of a home's regular roof shingles (rather than being mounted on top, as panels are).

This solution works well as long as there's enough sun for the panels to absorb and generate the needed energy. When there's not, the homeowner must use regular power (from their local electrical grid) or another alternative energy source.

Although owning or leasing solar panels can be an expensive proposition for homeowners, it does typically result in a fairly significant cost savings on the person's energy bill. Plus, it's an environmentally friendly alternative energy source.

When considering solar energy options, homeowners can either power their entire home with solar energy through photovoltaics or they can opt for a solar water heater that will only heat the water in the home—it won't provide electricity. As odd as it might sound, solar air conditioning is also an option, and it works similarly to solar water heating; it uses hot water in an air conditioning system, which means the homeowner no longer has to use electricity to run a traditional air conditioner.

Less common is the use of small wind turbines on residential homes. Particularly if a person owns a home that doesn't get a lot of sunlight (either because it's shaded by trees or because it's in a part of the country that doesn't get much sun), a wind turbine might be a better option. A small wind turbine can typically provide most of the power for the average home, although they do tend to be noisy and a bit of an eyesore.

Some people will take a smaller step toward using alternative energy at home and may build a solar oven. They're fairly easy to build out of everyday materials, and they can result in a decent energy savings if the person uses an oven frequently—traditional ovens require quite a bit of energy.

Most homeowners don't have a natural source of flowing water on their property, but those who do happen to have a river

Individuals can install small wind turbines to generate energy for their homes. Here, such a wind turbine is near a family home in China.

or stream can have a hydropower generator installed to capture the energy from the flowing water.

As mentioned in the previous chapter, some homeowners are now installing geothermal pumps on their property to use geothermal energy as a power source. The pumps for a single-family home require relatively little space, and the controllers now run on wireless technology, making them very convenient for homeowners.

Some homeowners also use stoves to burn biomass in the form of logs, chips, or pellets. Unlike burning coal, which emits carbon and contributes to air pollution, burning biomass is considered carbon-neutral—the carbon dioxide emitted when the biomass materials are burned is absorbed when the next crop of biomass is grown to produce fuel.

Even people who can't use any of these alternative energy sources in their own home can help save energy, though. By reducing the amount of electricity they use (by turning off unneeded lights, using energy-efficient lightbulbs, cooling the home by natural means rather than by running the air conditioner, and so on), they contribute to protecting the environment. Electricity is generated by various sources—some renewable, environmentally friendly alternative sources, but some fossil fuels and nonrenewable sources. The less electricity a person uses, the better the environmental impact on the planet. With the focus on environmental consciousness in the United States in recent decades, many Americans are taking this to heart and making efforts to curb their energy usage.

Driving Eco-Friendly Vehicles

Another way that Americans are preserving the planet is by switching from traditional gas-powered automobiles to hybrid

Vermont, a state known for its emphasis on the environment, uses plug-in hybrids for some of its state vehicles.

and electric cars. Conventional cars run on internal combustion or diesel engines, both of which contribute to pollution and both of which use crude oil, a fossil fuel. Eco-friendly cars, such as hybrids, electric cars, or cars that run on alternative fuels, reduce harmful emissions and also reduce dependence on crude oil.

There are various types of eco-friendly cars available. One of the earliest types widely available in the United States was the hybrid Toyota Prius. It was actually released in 2000, a year after the Honda Insight, another hybrid electric vehicle, but the Prius quickly overtook the Insight in terms of sales—possibly because its four-door sedan was more family-friendly than the two-door Insight. Priuses are still wildly popular today, and US sales figures report that more than 136,000 Priuses were sold in the United States in 2016. In fact, more than 40 percent of all hybrid vehicle sales in the United States are for the Prius. In total, more than 1.7 million Priuses have been sold in the United States since they were introduced in 2000.

There are other hybrid vehicles available now, too. Honda, Ford, Lexus, Hyundai, and Volkswagen all offer hybrids in the United States. In general, the technology for all is pretty similar—the car runs on both an internal combustion engine and a battery-powered drive system. Whenever possible, the battery power is

> ## fact!
> Of the roughly eleven million hybrid vehicles sold worldwide as of 2016, 45 percent of them were sold in Japan. The United States was responsible for 36 percent of sales, Europe about 14 percent of sales, and all other countries combined were responsible for the remaining roughly 5 percent.

Influence of Alternative Energy on Society

used, such as when pulling away from a stop and when idling at a stop. When needed, the car's engine will switch to fuel power and use the internal combustion engine.

Hybrids aren't the only eco-friendly vehicles, though. Electric cars are becoming more and more popular in the United States. They run completely on a rechargeable battery that powers an electric motor—no gas or diesel needed! Several manufacturers make electric cars, including Nissan, BMW, Chevrolet, Ford, and Tesla. Chevrolet makes the best-selling electric car in the United States, with its Volt plug-in hybrid. However, the Volt is a hybrid—it does partially rely on a conventional internal combustion engine. The best-selling all-electric car in the United States is the Nissan Leaf, which *only* runs on electricity. The Tesla Model S comes in third—perhaps in part because it is more than twice as expensive as the Leaf!

As of late 2016, more than 570,000 electric cars had been sold in the United States since 2008, when Tesla launched its Roadster. Nearly half of those sales have been in California, which boasts 48 percent of all electric car sales between 2011 and mid-2016. According to Bloomberg New Energy Finance, increased battery production over the next several years will result in the price for electric cars decreasing, and by 2030 electric cars may be less expensive than traditional cars with internal combustion engines.

A more recent entry into the eco-friendly vehicle market is hydrogen-powered cars. These convert hydrogen gas into electricity to power the car via a fuel cell. Compared to conventional gas- or diesel-fueled cars, they produce no tailpipe emissions and reduced global-warming emissions. Consumers refill the hydrogen gas at a filling station, just like one refuels a conventional car—but of course, the filling station must offer hydrogen gas!

Tesla, Elon Musk, and Beyond

Tesla has become a household name in recent years, thanks in part to its production of luxury electric vehicles, including the Roadster and the Model S. But Tesla is actually more than just an automaker. Founded in 2003 and based in Palo Alto, California, Tesla now makes cars, solar panels, and lithium-ion battery energy storage.

Probably the most famous face of the company is Elon Musk, a South African-born engineer and inventor who also founded SpaceX, Neuralink, SolarCity, Zip2, and X.com (which ultimately became PayPal). Musk's goals for many of his companies include using sustainable energy production and consumption to help reduce global warming. For example, Tesla produces electric cars, and SolarCity offers solar energy products and storage.

Musk's ambitions spread beyond Earth, though; Musk founded SpaceX as a first step toward his ultimate goal of colonizing Mars.

Hydrogen cars are not widely available as of this writing, but there are three models available in certain US markets: one by Toyota, one by Hyundai, and one by Honda. Other companies are working on developing models of hydrogen cars, but how quickly they will be adopted into the US market remains to be seen. Although hydrogen cars produce no tailpipe emissions, there are high carbon emissions produced during the process of converting natural gas to hydrogen. In fact, some experts believe that the process of converting natural gas to hydrogen produces *more* pollution than simply running conventional gas-powered cars.

The conversion process not only produces carbon emissions, it is also currently very expensive. Scientists are working on alternative methods for creating hydrogen fuel, but so far they are even costlier than the process of converting natural gas to hydrogen.

It would also be quite costly to build facilities to provide hydrogen fuel for vehicles. Right now, fuel stations are unlikely to want to invest in building those facilities because there aren't enough consumers driving hydrogen vehicles to make it financially worth their while. Also, the fuel cells needed for hydrogen cars are quite expensive.

Skeptics suggest that it's not worthwhile to spend time and energy on further developing hydrogen cars because it will take decades to make them widely available, and that time could be better spent refining hybrid- and electric-vehicle technologies. In 2007, US Department of Energy official Joseph Romm, a renowned physicist, climate expert, and environmental author, stated that hydrogen cars would "not [be available] in our lifetime, and very possibly never."

Beyond all this technology for making eco-friendly cars, there's another way that Americans have been influenced by the alternative energy movement: more and more Americans are biking to work or school, or taking mass transit, such as buses, subways, and trains. From 1995 to 2013, public transportation ridership reportedly increased by more than 37 percent, according to the American Public Transportation Association. The Pew Research Center revealed in 2016 that 11 percent of Americans reported they take public transportation on a daily or weekly basis. Between 2004 and 2014, the number of people biking to work grew by more than 60 percent, according to the US Census Bureau, with approximately 786,000 American reporting in 2012 that they biked to work. Because many forms of public transportation now use alternative energy sources, this has had a positive environmental impact over decades past, when Americans were more inclined to use their gas-powered cars for transportation.

Governmental Responses to the Alternative Energy Movement

The need for alternative energy sources that will reduce pollution and preserve natural resources is widely recognized as extremely important by individuals and by the government. That is not to say it's supported by *everyone*—there are individuals and government officials who dismiss or even deny climate change and don't feel the need to make efforts to increase the use of environmentally friendly alternatives. However, in general, the movement has gained wide support, and the majority of the government recognizes it as an important issue.

Because of this, governments have introduced incentives, rebates, and tax credits to encourage citizens to adopt environmentally friendly solutions in their home and for their transportation. Some of these incentives, rebates, and credits are offered at the state or even local level, which means they will vary by state and locality. State and local government websites generally offer information about such credits and incentives on their website. Interested persons can also consult the US Department of Energy website, which has a page where they can search by state to find available savings programs and incentives.

Not surprisingly, some states have more government-sponsored programs and credits available than others. Large states like California and Texas have many pages of possible credits and exemptions, whereas small and sparsely populated states like Rhode Island and Wyoming have far fewer.

Up until the end of 2016, the federal government offered incentives for installing and using environmentally friendly heating, cooling, and water heating products; small wind electric systems; geothermal heat pumps; and fuel cells. However, those incentives expired at the end of 2016. The presidential administration of 2017 did not appear to place a strong focus on encouraging environmental conservation—in fact, there was great debate about climate change after President Donald Trump's remarks that climate change was a hoax. However, today a federal tax credit for solar energy systems is still in force: it expires at the end of 2021. There are also federal tax credits available for plug-in hybrid cars and all-electric cars (often as well as state and local credits for these purchases). There is also a mortgage program called an energy-efficient mortgage (EEM) that helps people interested in buying energy-efficient homes finance their purchase. The mortgage program is also available for people who buy older homes and do renovations that result in an energy-efficient home.

The federal government also offers tax credits to small businesses that make energy-efficient upgrades. There are federal

The Greenest States

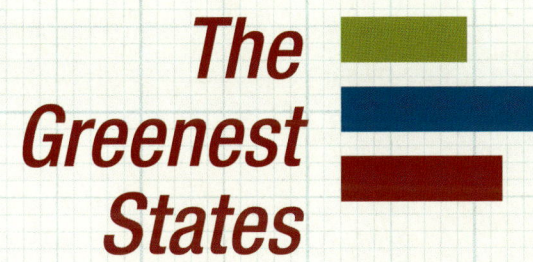

In 2017, analysts did a study on the greenest (that is, the most environmentally friendly) states in the United States. They considered twenty **metrics**, such as share of energy consumption from renewable resources and number of **LEED**-certified buildings per capita, when determining the environmental quality of each state and the eco-friendliness of its policies. Overall, they found Vermont, Massachusetts, Oregon, Washington, and Connecticut to be the top five greenest states, while Oklahoma, North Dakota, West Virginia, Montana, and Wyoming rounded out the bottom five.

It's interesting that California did not crack the top five—it came in at number thirteen overall. California has long been well known for its focus on the environment and environmentally friendly solutions. In fact, California came in fourth in the "eco-friendly behaviors" category. However, it came in a dismal forty-third in the "environmental quality" category, which dragged its overall rank down. This makes sense: as much as Californians tend to be very in tune with environmental issues, the state *does* have a significant problem with air pollution and is very often in a state of drought.

tax credits for home builders who construct energy-efficient homes, credits for manufacturers who produce energy-efficient appliances, and tax deductions for commercial building owners and **lessees** who install energy-efficient lighting, heating, cooling, ventilation, and hot water systems.

In addition to providing credits and incentives to individuals and businesses that implement energy-saving measures, many governments themselves have implemented environmentally friendly and energy-saving measures. For example, in 2015, Burlington, Vermont, became the first city in the United States to use 100 percent renewable energy for its forty-two thousand citizens' electricity, harnessed from wind, solar, biomass, and hydroelectric sources. In addition to preserving resources and reducing pollutants from using fossil fuels, this switch to 100 percent renewable energy is forecast to save the city of Burlington approximately $20 million over twenty years.

Another place the government has been making use of alternative energy is in the prison system. In 2011, the National Institute of Corrections, a part of the US Department of Justice, issued a report entitled "The Greening of Corrections: Creating a Sustainable System." The report was intended to help correctional facilities understand practical strategies for becoming more self-sustaining and less damaging to the environment. As Director of the National Institute of Corrections Morris Thigpen wrote:

> Increasingly, correctional professionals are evaluating the long-term impacts of corrections buildings, operations, and programs on the environment, community, and economy, and are establishing sustainability plans and green practices ... The benefits of greening correctional facilities are both short and long term; they will consume fewer resources, create less pollution, and provide healthier

environments for the users—inmates, staff, visitors, and administration. A sustainable model of corrections also goes beyond facilities and operations and should be tied to a comprehensive strategy that provides access to viable hands-on training and job opportunities for inmates to reduce **recidivism** and influence them to become productive citizens in an emerging green economy.

In other words, greening correctional facilities has multiple benefits. It is environmentally conscious, but it can also provide a job-training opportunity for inmates to give them a path to a productive, legal life when they are released from prison.

Other government departments and agencies have taken similar steps toward operating in a more environmentally conscious manner, too. Schools, for example, often incorporate environmentally friendly practices on their campuses. Some schools have installed solar panels over parking spaces to harness the sun's energy while shading cars in the lot. Many have put in school gardens, which help reduce pollution by reducing the amount of carbon dioxide in the air and increasing the amount of oxygen. Most schools now separate trash and recyclables as well. Under Bill Clinton's presidency in the 1990s, the White House launched a Greening of the White House initiative designed to use more renewable resources, reduce waste, and lower energy consumption at the famous home.

Corporate and Business Responses to the Alternative Energy Movement

Many businesses have also responded favorably to the alternative energy movement, making upgrades to energy-efficient solutions where possible. Their motivation may be concern for the environment or it may be to take advantage of an incentive or tax credit—or, more likely, a bit of both—but regardless, the result is that many businesses and corporations now look to alternative and environmentally friendly energy sources and solutions. Certainly, many businesses devoted to the alternative energy movement have sprung up, such as solar panel manufacturers, geothermal pump manufacturers, home builders dedicated to building energy-efficient homes, and so on.

In April 2017, clean energy businesses in Minnesota banded together to **lobby** the Minnesota legislature in what they called Minnesota's first ever Clean Energy Business Day. It's not unusual for like-minded businesses and advocates to join together and lobby state legislatures or even Congress in a so-called "day on the Hill," but this was the first time clean energy businesses had done so in Minnesota. The Minnesota legislature was considering a number of actions not friendly to clean energy businesses, such as killing a fund devoted to solar manufacturing and renewable development, so the businesses and advocates took action. Minnesota has a renewable energy standard of 25 percent for the state's utilities, which has created fifty-four thousand jobs in approximately eight hundred firms in the state. The businesses were lobbying to increase that standard to 50 percent, which they felt would help more clean energy businesses invest in Minnesota and would create more jobs in the industry.

In addition, many large businesses in the United States have committed to using renewable energy sources as much as possible. In late 2016, the Climate Reality Project, founded by Nobel Laureate and former United States vice president Al Gore, recognized five companies that have done a particularly good job of switching to clean energy.

The first is technology giant Intel, which was also number one on the EPA's Green Power Partnership National Top 100 list in 2017. Intel has been the top voluntary corporate purchaser of green power in the United States for the past eight years, meeting 100 percent of its electricity use in the United States in 2015 with purchased renewable power from wind, solar, geothermal, biomass, and hydropower sources. The company has solar plants on several of its facilities, and it also has a wind farm on the top of its headquarters in California.

The second recognized company is Kohl's, which has been the number one green power–using retailer in the United States since 2009, according to the EPA's Green Power Partnership Top 30 Retail list. Nearly all of its stores in forty-nine states are **Energy Star**–certified, and more than 10 percent have on-site solar panels installed. Kohl's also made a name as the first retailer in the United States to have a carbon-neutral goal in partnership with the EPA—a goal they have met since 2010.

The third recognized entity is the National Hockey League (NHL), which in 2015 became the first professional sports organization or league to earn a spot on the EPA's Green Power Partnership National Top 100 list. It earned seventeenth place among the largest users of green power in the United States. Since 2014, the NHL has also counterbalanced all greenhouse gas emissions from its activities, and since 2011 it has restored more than 50 million gallons (189 million liters) of fresh water to rivers and streams in North America.

The fourth recognized business might come as a surprise: Walmart. Walmart has been vilified over the years as a corporate giant paying low wages and putting smaller mom-and-pop stores out of business. Whether or not that's true, it's a fact that Walmart is a very environmentally conscious corporation. Walmart has been a Green Power Partner with the EPA since 2009 and has a goal to use 100 percent renewable power by 2020, while also achieving zero waste and curbing its greenhouse gas emissions.

Walmart is also one of the leading corporate installers of solar energy systems. For four years in a row, Walmart grabbed the top spot on the Solar Energy Industries Association's list of leading corporate solar installer in the United States. In 2016, it came in second only to Target.

The fifth recognized company is Apple, which in 2016 joined the RE100 Initiative—a collaboration of businesses committed to relying on 100 percent renewable energy. In April 2017, the tech giant finished building a massive new campus in California that it intends to power by 100 percent renewable energy—primarily harnessed from a massive on-site corporate solar installation. Although it may sound like an ambitious goal, it's one Apple is likely to meet, given that it already uses 100 percent renewable energy to power its operations in the United States, China, and twenty-one other countries.

There are many other smaller businesses and corporations that have also committed to using alternative, renewable energy as much as possible—too many to name, in fact. Clearly, much of the corporate and business world has recognized the importance of alternative energy for saving our planet.

Companies Going Green

Today, many companies are choosing to adopt green energy. Numbers one to ten on the EPA's Green Power Partnership National Top 100 list for 2017 are:

1. Intel
2. Microsoft
3. Google
4. Kohl's
5. Bank of America
6. Apple
7. Cisco
8. The City of Houston, Texas
9. Starbucks
10. The US Department of Energy.

That's right—Starbucks uses more green power than the US Department of Energy!

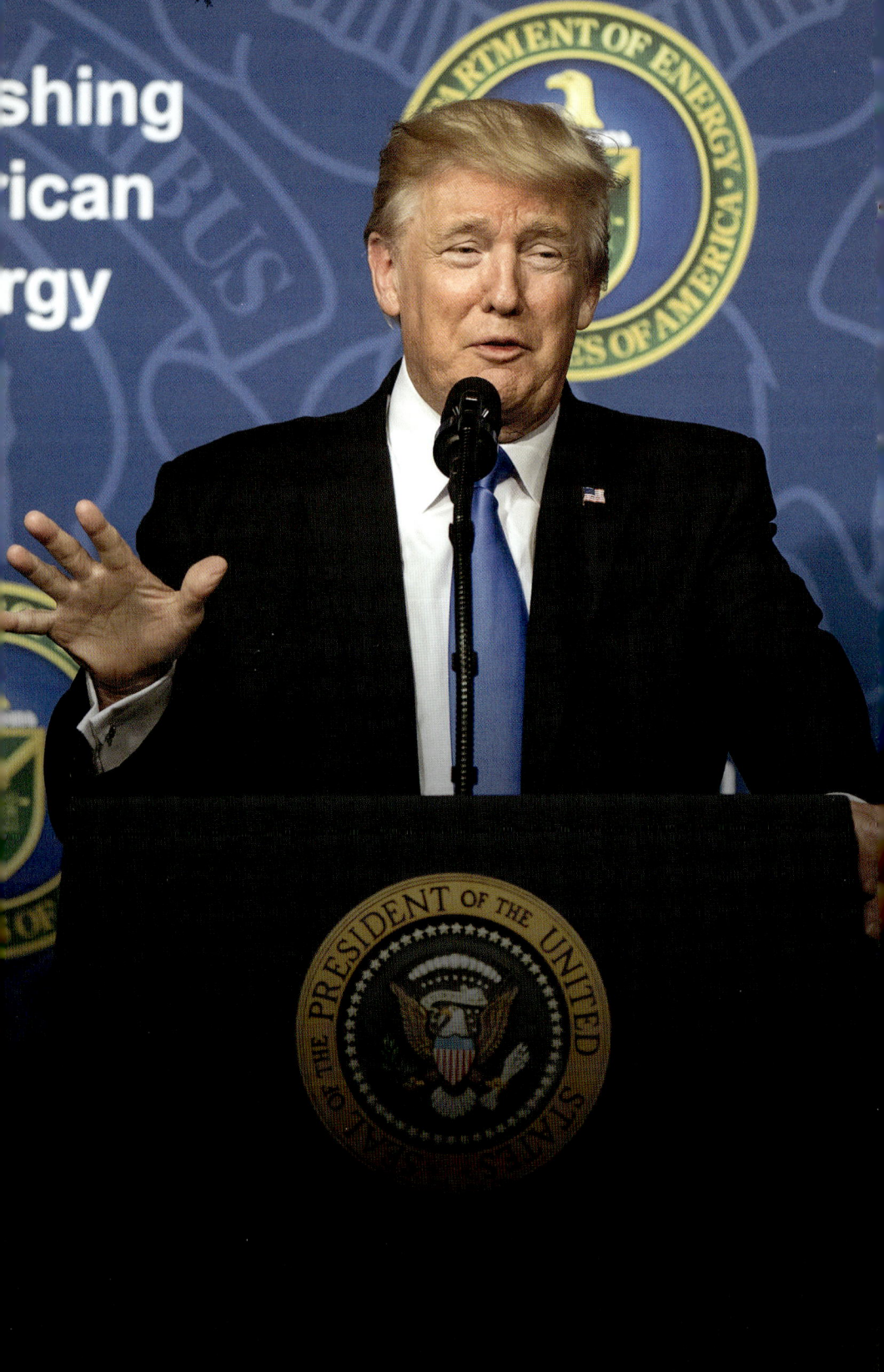

4

Challenges to the Alternative Energy Movement

While a great number of people in the United States, many businesses and corporations, and many governments and government agencies support the alternative energy movement and support the need to move away from using fossil fuels to using green power, there are detractors to the movement out there. In fact, the movement has faced a fair amount of setbacks since 2017, with opposition from the Trump administration, which is disappointing to those who applauded the Obama administration for its focus on environmental issues.

Facing Challenges

Some environmental measures come from individuals, and those aren't usually affected by the political climate. Homeowners interested in putting solar panels on their homes aren't going to change their minds based on who is in the White House.

Opposite: US president Donald Trump spoke during an energy conference in June 2017. His goal is for the country to focus on "American energy dominance" rather than fighting climate change.

Some environmentally focused changes and solutions come at the local and state levels of government. These plans are not always touched by changes in federal administration, either. If a local government wants to offer homeowners some sort of incentive for installing a wind turbine at their home, for example, that's a local decision and not likely to be very affected by the federal government.

However, there's a certain trickledown from the federal government in many things. Often federal legislation for a particular topic exists, but its implementation is left to state governments. As an example, consider an educational act: the Every Student Succeeds Act (ESSA). This is a federal statute, but the federal government allows states to decide how it is carried out. Every state must comply with ESSA, but how they choose to do so is up to the state. Therefore, not every state will implement ESSA in the same way.

The same is true with pretty much any type of legislation. There are certain laws and policies that are administered at the federal level, but there are others that are passed down to states, who then decide how to implement them. Often, it's a combination of both federal and state oversight, too—some laws will be at the federal level, and others will be at the state level.

The Clean Air Act is a great example. It's federal legislation, but the EPA works with federal and state regulatory partners to ensure that each state is complying with the laws and regulations put in place at the state and federal levels to uphold the Clean Air Act. It's easy to see, then, how a presidential administration and Congress can influence something like the alternative energy movement. If the president and Congress don't put a priority on programs designed to support the alternative energy movement, the movement will falter.

The Obama Years

President Barack Obama and his administration were known for being very supportive of environmental causes and the alternative energy movement. At the 2014 United Nations Climate Change Summit, President Obama stated, "There's one issue that will define the contours of this century more dramatically than any other, and that is the urgent and growing threat of a changing climate."

Indeed, President Obama tried to help transition the United States into a more environmentally sustainable nation that would not contribute to climate change. The *Washington Post* said that Obama "could also be dubbed the 'energy efficiency president'—the US leader who has done more than any other to help us use less energy, and pay less for it, as we go about our daily lives. Which, of course, also helps fight climate change." Jamie Henn, cofounder of environmental activist organization 350.org, stated that "Obama did more than any other president before him, but it still wasn't enough." That's in large part because Obama faced obstacles of a resistant, largely Republican Congress and a lack of cooperation from other world leaders. Climate change is a global problem, so one single nation can't reverse it. It requires cooperation from virtually every country.

Still, Obama made many important contributions to the movement. For example, he championed COP21, the Paris Climate Agreement, which was the first climate agreement in which countries globally agreed to reduce carbon emissions. He also issued an executive order attempting to regulate coal emissions from power plants (although his executive order was blocked by the Supreme Court). He imposed new, tighter regulations on automobile emissions in 2009, which reportedly had a significant impact on per capita automobile emissions.

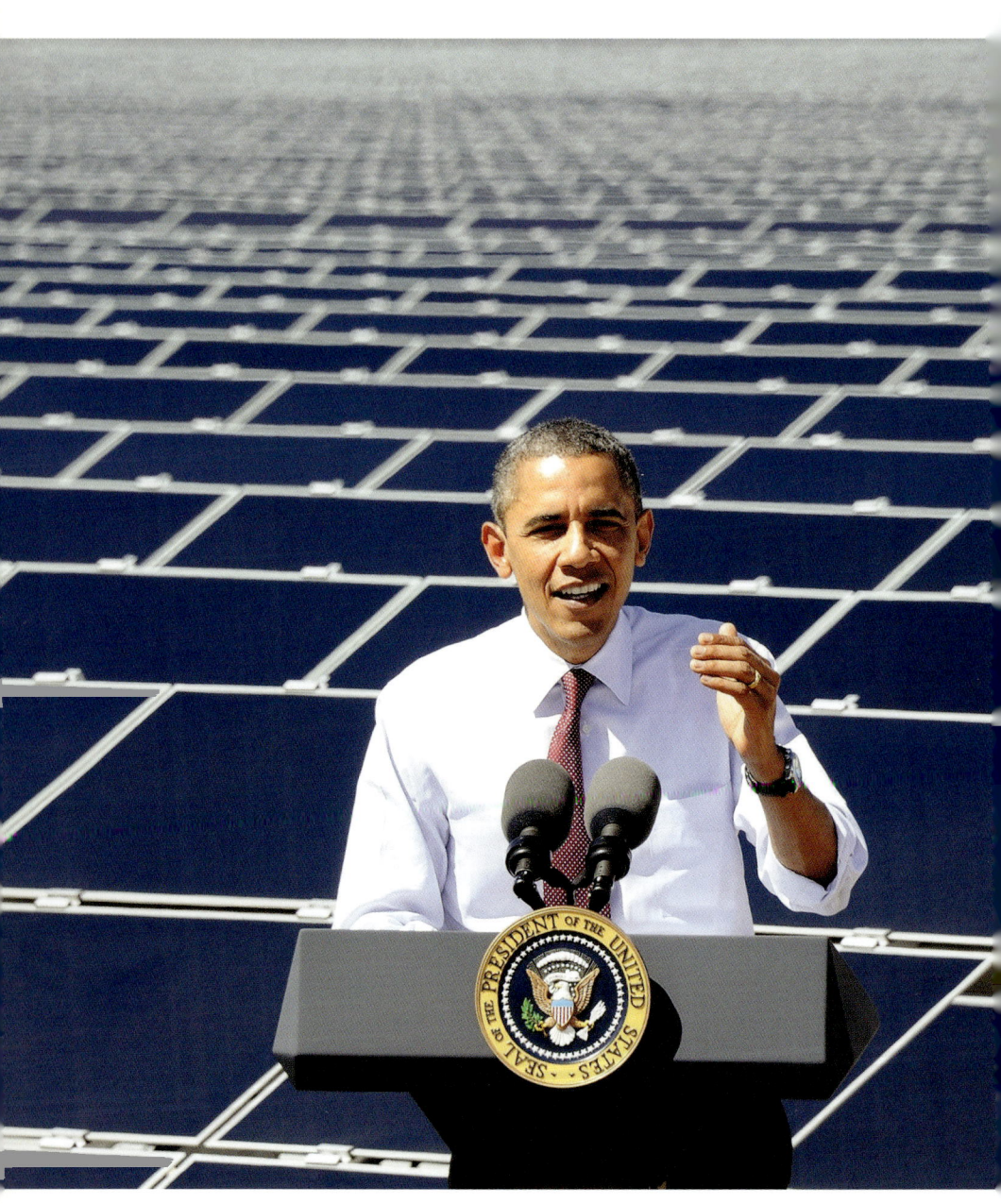

On a four-state tour to promote his alternative energy policies in 2012, President Barack Obama visited the United States' largest photovoltaic solar plant, located in Boulder City, Nevada.

He pressed appliance manufacturers to improve the efficiency standards of their products. He invested billions in renewable energy—under the Obama administration, the US Department of Energy invested more than $30 billion in renewable energy, and a White House–led coalition of private sector investors invested more than $4 billion.

Obama also issued a policy called the Clean Power Plan, which was broadly aimed at combatting climate change by reducing carbon dioxide emissions from power plants and by increasing the use of renewable energy sources and conserving energy.

The Trump Years

When President Donald Trump took office in early 2017, within weeks he had signed an executive order on energy independence. This called for the Clean Power Plan to be reviewed. President Trump's order addressing the Clean Power Plan was thought to be an attempt to deliver on his promise of bringing back jobs in the coal industry. The coal industry had been declining for years, which put laborers out of work in places like West Virginia, where coal was once a dominant industry.

fact!

The Paris Agreement went into effect on November 4, 2016. The agreement was signed by 192 states and the European Union, and 147 of those parties ratified the agreement, including the United States, China, and India, who made up three of the top four greenhouse gas emitters. (Russia was the fourth, and it had signed the agreement, though not ratified it.) However, in 2017, US president Trump announced the United States would withdraw from the agreement by 2020.

Trump felt that the strict regulations in the Clean Power Plan were part of what forced miners out of work, and he aimed to roll back regulations so that coal mines and coal-fired power plants could continue to operate, thus bringing back jobs.

fact!

While no one would argue that unemployment is a problem and jobs are good, supporters of the alternative energy movement feared that rolling back regulations would damage the environment and the planet—eventually beyond repair.

In March 2017, the Trump administration released the first draft of its 2018 budget, called "A New Foundation for American Greatness." Initially, it slashed the budget of the EPA by 31 percent, more than any other government agency. It eliminated programs designed to restore several large bodies of water, such as the Great Lakes and Puget Sound. It also cut funding for cleanup of **Superfund sites** and reduced the Department of Energy budget by 6 percent.

One positive note for green energy advocates is that presidential power is not unchecked. Even if President Trump wanted to dismantle *all*

> A 2016 Pew Research Center survey showed that only 58 percent of Republicans felt that environmental laws and regulations were too strict, to the detriment of the economy. By comparison, only 17 percent of Democrats felt that way. In other words, more than three-quarters of Democrats and nearly half of Republicans do *not* believe that strict environmental laws and regulations have cost people jobs and hurt the economy.

While many Americans worry about climate change and the effect President Trump's policies will have on our environmental future, people working in the coal industry are pleased by his promises to bring back coal as an energy source and thus create more jobs.

environmental policies put in place by recent years, Congress would have to agree. While the Democratic Party is generally known for being friendlier to environmental issues, there are many members of the Republican Party who recognize the reality and dangers of climate change and will, in theory, work to continue to protect the environment and support alternative energy sources. For example, in May 2017, the US Senate voted against a measure to repeal Obama's regulations on methane emissions. The Republican-controlled House of Representatives voted to pass the measure, but the Senate rejected it, which means that Obama's regulations on venting and flaring of natural gas from oil and gas facilities on US Bureau of Land Management lands will remain in place. This was an important victory for environmentally conscious people because methane actually poses an even greater climate threat than carbon dioxide—it has twenty-five times the global warming capacity of carbon dioxide.

Another positive note for environmentalists is that given the Trump administration's perceived lack of interest in moving forward with environmentally friendly policies and regulations, many states have strengthened their commitment to enforcing environmental policies and regulations at the state level. According to Dallas Burtraw, from the think tank Resources for the Future, "There are state policies that are strong throughout the nation, but especially in the northeast states, in California and a number of other states, we see leadership on climate and energy policies … A number of other states have climate policy goals already articulated. They take shape mostly in the form of clean energy policies with over half the states in the country having funded energy efficiency standards." In other words, even if a presidential administration doesn't particularly support the advancement or use of alternative energy sources, that doesn't mean the end of the movement. Individuals, businesses, and local and state governments can still continue to move it forward.

A Surprising Pick for EPA Head

When president-elect Donald Trump began choosing the people who would make up his cabinet, environmentalists and many other citizens were shocked by his pick for the head of the EPA: Scott Pruitt, the attorney general of Oklahoma. Pruitt had, in the past, referred to himself as a "leading advocate against the EPA's activist agenda." He had repeatedly sued the EPA and other related government entities, sometimes doing so in cooperation with fossil fuel companies. In May 2016, he wrote, "Scientists continue to disagree about the degree and extent of global warming and its connection to the actions of mankind," when the vast majority of climate and environmental scientists agree that human-caused climate change is in fact real—and is a threat to the future of the planet. In other words, Pruitt was not seen as a particular friend to the environment. Despite all of this, in February 2017, the Senate confirmed Pruitt as the new head of the EPA.

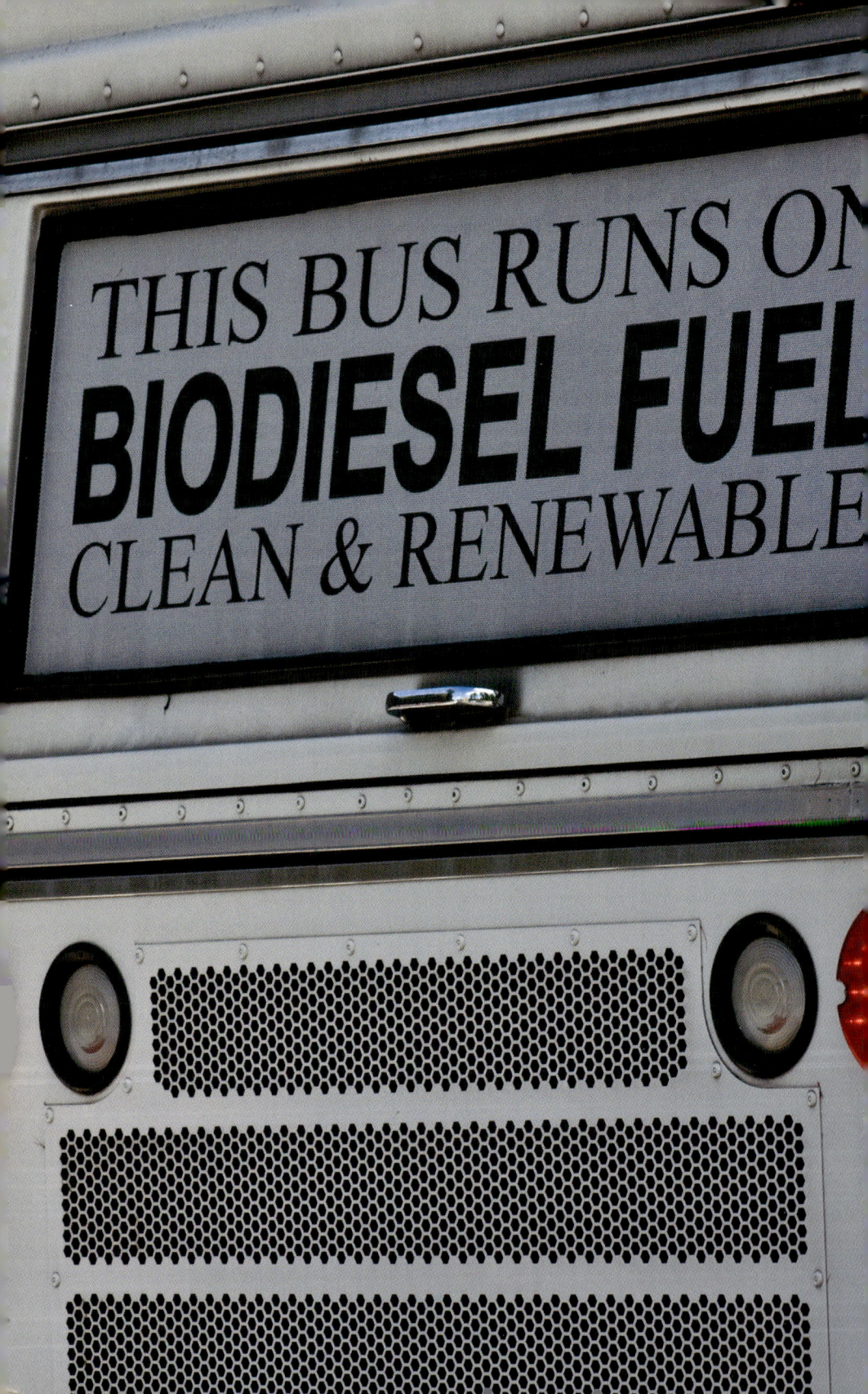

5

The Legacy of the Alternative Energy Movement

Although the future of the alternative energy movement is somewhat uncertain, one thing is for sure: the movement will continue in some way, shape, or form. Many states and local municipalities have pledged to continue research and development into switching increasingly to alternative energy sources. The vast majority of climate scientists recognize that climate change is a pressing issue and will continue to pursue resources and technologies to preserve the planet. And then there are individual people, who as a collective group can make a major difference.

The Role of Individuals in the Future of the Alternative Energy Movement

According to a 2016 Pew Research Center survey, 74 percent of adults in the United States think "the country should do whatever

Opposite: More and more cities are adopting alternative energy–fueled vehicles for their public transportation systems.

This Dutch solar-powered car is an example of the forward-thinking energy solutions being explored around the world.

it takes to protect the environment." Seventy-four percent! That means in a room with ten people, at least seven of them will be in favor of environmental protection. With the United States population hovering around 325 million, that means roughly 240 million people are in favor of protecting the environment. One person might make a small impact, but 240 million people could make a *big* impact.

The key word here is "could," though. A 2016 Pew Research Center survey demonstrated that although roughly three-quarters of US adults are concerned about helping the environment, only about one in five actually makes a consistent effort on a regular basis to do so. Of those who said they consistently make the effort to protect the environment, 36 percent were adults age sixty-five and older, while only 12 percent were adults age eighteen to twenty-nine.

In other words, young adults can step up their efforts to protect the environment—and actually, they are the perfect age group to do so. Most adults between the ages of eighteen and twenty-nine are commuting either to school or to work, and considering environmentally friendly methods of transportation is one very positive step people can make to protect the environment. They can choose to bike to work or take public transportation, which is increasingly more likely to use alternative energy sources.

Making Smart Transportation Choices

Fewer cars on the road mean less pollution and a cleaner environment, and a great many buses run on alternative energy sources—far more than cars. Research done by the American Public Transportation Association (APTA) showed that as of early 2014, 41.3 percent of public transportation buses in the United States ran on alternative fuels or used hybrid technology—

More and more individuals are installing solar panels at their home.

compared to just 4.2 percent of cars that used alternative fuels or flex-fuel. Of the public-transit buses used in the United States, 16.9 percent were hybrid-electric as of 2014, and 16.7 percent used compressed natural gas, liquefied natural gas, and blends. Biodiesel-fueled buses made up 7.4 percent of the US fleet, and buses running on other alternative fuels, such as propane and hydrogen, made up 0.3 percent of the public-transit buses in the United States.

The president of the APTA commented in 2015, "The public transportation industry is a leader in sustainability, committed to incorporating green, sustainable practices whenever possible. This commitment is demonstrated in many ways, including the use of alternative fuel and alternate-powered buses, LEED-certified buildings, and solar arrays."

If biking or taking public transit isn't an option for a person, they can always opt to purchase or lease an eco-friendly vehicle, such as a hybrid or an electric car. Electric vehicles can be charged at a person's home, and there were also more than twelve thousand public charging stations available in the United States as of early 2016—a number that is continuing to grow.

Making Smart Living Choices

In addition to making environmentally conscious choices in transportation, people can make eco-friendly choices in their living environment. The costs for installing environmentally friendly energy sources such as solar panels, wind turbines, and geothermal pumps are continuing to decrease and become more affordable for homeowners.

Even renters and people living with roommates or their parents can make environmentally conscious decisions about their living environment. Air-drying clothes instead of using an energy-consuming clothes dryer is an option during warmer, non-rainy months. Manufacturers with an eye toward environmental

> *fact!*
>
> Whether public transit is a viable option for people largely depends on where they live. Larger metropolitan areas tend to have better-developed transit systems. According to a 2016 study based on data from the US Census Bureau, the five best US cities for public transit are Washington, DC; San Francisco, California; Boston, Massachusetts; Chicago, Illinois; and New York, New York.

consciousness offer numerous nonelectric appliances for people who want to live "off the grid," such as solar ovens and solar camp showers.

For those who don't want to live completely off the grid, there are environmentally friendly appliances, such as those with the Energy Star rating, which the EPA created in 1992 to identify energy-efficient products, homes, and buildings. There are simple steps anyone can take to save energy, such as turning off unused lights, resisting the temptation to turn on the air conditioner the moment it gets warm, using an extra sweater or blanket instead of immediately turning on the heater, and limiting the use of hot water when possible.

> *fact!*
>
> For people who want to live off the grid, sustainable communities have been springing up across the United States, in places such as Oregon, New Mexico, North Carolina, California, Missouri, and Virginia. Some of these communities rely on hydropower, solar power, and geothermal wells for their energy needs.

Looking to the Future

As we look toward the future, experts say moving forward with a continued focus on preserving Earth's natural resources and limiting the pollutants released into the air are ultimately the best ways to ensure the long-term viability of the planet. A focus on continuing to research and implement alternative energy solutions is the perfect legacy to leave to future generations.

Kids Saving the Environment

Students may not be in a position to purchase alternative-fuel vehicles or install solar panels on their family homes, but there's plenty they *can* do to help protect the planet. GreenMyParents is a nationwide program that helps kids and teens teach their parents and their peers how to save the planet through everyday actions. They have a book, *Green My Parents*, a strong presence on social media, and public workshops held around the country. The GMP Youth movement works with the EPA, the Energy Star program, the National Wildlife Federation, and many other like-minded organizations to promote environmental practices. Kids for a Clean Environment (Kids FACE) is another national organization that promotes youth involvement in environmental action; they have more than three hundred thousand members around the world. KidsEcoClub offers classroom and after-school environmental clubs and activities to encourage hands-on environmental learning and leadership opportunities for kids.

Glossary

biofuel A fuel that comes from living matter.

Bronze Age A time period of early urban civilization characterized by the use of bronze. The period went from roughly 3300 BCE to 600 BCE.

climate change A change in global climate patterns thought to be caused by higher levels of pollutants produced by the burning of fossil fuels.

coal gasification A process by which synthetic gas is produced using coal and water, air, and/or oxygen.

crude oil Unrefined petroleum.

electrical grid A network that delivers electricity from suppliers to consumers.

Energy Star An EPA program that certifies products and buildings that meet certain energy-efficiency standards.

fossil fuel A natural fuel formed from the remains of living organisms. Fossil fuels include coal and gas.

fracking A process by which pressurized liquid is injected into subterranean rocks to force open cracks and extract oil or gas.

global warming The gradual increase in the temperature of Earth's atmosphere, believed to be caused by increased levels of pollutants in the air.

greenhouse gases Gases that contribute to the greenhouse effect (global warming) by absorbing infrared radiation. Carbon dioxide is one greenhouse gas.

Hellenistic period A period of ancient Greek and Mediterranean history that spans roughly 323 BCE to 31 BCE.

hydrokinetic Related to the motion of water or fluid.

kerosene Fuel oil made by distilling petroleum. It is often used in jet engines and portable lamps.

knots A unit of speed used for ships, aircraft, and the wind.

LEED An acronym for Leadership in Energy and Environmental Design, a rating system that evaluates a building's environmental performance.

lessee A person who leases, or rents, a property.

lobby An attempt to influence a politician or administration about an issue.

mantle The layer of Earth between the crust and the core.

metrics Measuring factors.

Neolithic period A time period at the end of the Stone Age characterized by the development of human technology. It spanned roughly 10,000 BCE to 2000 BCE.

Paleolithic period A prehistoric period characterized by the development and use of primitive stone tools.

photon A particle that carries energy and represents a quantum of light or other electromagnetic radiation.

photovoltaics Devices that produce an electrical current at the junction of two substances exposed to light.

polymer A substance made of a large number of similar units bonded together, such as in plastics and resins.

recidivism The tendency of someone who has committed a crime to commit another crime.

semiconductor A substance that has conductivity between an insulator and most other metals. Semiconductors are an essential component of most electronic circuits.

Superfund site Former toxic-waste dump sites that are being cleaned up.

tectonic plate A massive slab of rock that lies on top of Earth's mantle.

vortices Whirling masses of fluid.

Further Information

Books

Cunningham, Anne C. *Critical Perspectives on Fossil Fuels vs. Renewable Energy.* New York: Enslow Publishing, 2017.

Green, Robert. *How Renewable Energy Is Changing Society.* San Diego, CA: ReferencePoint Press, 2015.

Haugen, David M. *Energy Alternatives.* Farmington Hills, MI: Greenhaven Press, 2010.

Zuchora-Walske, Christine. *Solar Energy.* Minneapolis, MN: Essential Library, 2013.

Websites

Office of Energy Efficiency and Renewable Energy
https://energy.gov/eere/office-energy-efficiency-renewable-energy

The website for this Department of Energy office is full of useful information for people who want to know more about renewable energy options and energy efficiency.

Renewable Energy World
http://www.renewableenergyworld.com

This comprehensive website is full of the latest news about renewable energy.

Videos

Modern Marvels Renewable Energy
https://www.youtube.com/watch?v=0k1GPOUlqqs

The History Channel's *Modern Marvels* offers a thought-provoking look at renewable energy.

Twenty-First Century Renewable Energy
https://www.youtube.com/watch?v=8uyHAPrIFxw

This YouTube page has a fascinating documentary about renewable energy in the twenty-first century.

What's the Best Form of Alternative Energy?
https://www.youtube.com/watch?v=tJFl2roZB0Q

Science Plus put together this fifteen-minute video discussing what they consider the best forms of alternative energy.

Organizations

Sierra Club
http://www.sierraclub.org

The Sierra Club is devoted to protecting the planet, and its website provides a wealth of information about how you can get involved.

Sustainable Summer
http://www.sustainablesummer.org

This organization helps teens interested in working for a greener world find summer programs.

US Environmental Protection Agency
http://www.epa.gov

The website for the United States Environmental Protection Agency is full of news about different current environmental issues.

Bibliography

Anderson, Monica. "For Earth Day, Here's How Americans View Environmental Issues." Pew Research Center. April 20, 2017. http://www.pewresearch.org/fact-tank/2017/04/20/for-earth-day-heres-how-americans-view-environmental-issues.

Bedard, Roger, et al. "North American Ocean Energy Status – March 2007." Proceedings of the Seventh European Wave and Tidal Energy Conference. September 11–13, 2007. Porto, Portugal.

Boyd, Robert S. "Hydrogen Cars May Be a Long Time Coming." McClatchy DC Bureau. May 15, 2007. http://www.mcclatchydc.com/news/nation-world/national/article24463207.html.

Bullis, Kevin. "Adaptive Material Could Cut the Cost of Solar in Half." *MIT Technology Review*. July 30, 2014. https://www.technologyreview.com/s/529476/adaptive-material-could-cut-the-cost-of-solar-in-half.

Cobb, Jeff. "Americans Buy Their Four-Millionth Hybrid Car." Hybrid Cars. June 6, 2016. http://www.hybridcars.com/americans-buy-their-four-millionth-hybrid-car.

Crisp, D., A. Pathare, and R. C. Ewell. "The Performance of Gallium Arsenide/Germanium Solar Cells at the Martian Surface." *Acta Astronautica*. Vol. 54, Issue 2. p. 83–101.

Dimroth, Frank. "Four-Junction Wafer Bonded Concentrator Solar Cells." *IEEE Journal of Photovoltaics*. Vol, 6, Issue 1. January 2016. p. 343. http://ieeexplore.ieee.org/stamp/stamp.jsp?arnumber=7342876.

"Electricity: Recent Data." US Energy Information Administration. https://www.eia.gov/electricity.

"Energy Dept: New Wind Energy Technology Unlocks Wind Development Opportunity in All 50 States." American Wind Energy Association. May 19, 2015. http://www.awea.org/MediaCenter/pressrelease.aspx?ItemNumber=7614.

"Five Major Businesses Powered by Renewable Energy." Climate Reality Project. November 25, 2016. https://www.climaterealityproject.org/blog/5-major-businesses-powered-renewable-energy.

"41% of U.S. Public Transit Buses Use Alt Fuels, Hybrid Technology." *Metro Magazine*. April 17, 2015. http://www.metro-magazine.com/sustainability/news/293950/41-of-u-s-public-transit-buses-use-alt-fuels-hybrid-technology.

Green, Martin A. *Third Generation Photovoltaics: Advanced Solar Energy Conversion*. New York: Springer, 2003.

"The Greening of Corrections: Creating a Sustainable System." National Institute of Corrections. March 2011. http://static.nicic.gov/Library/024914.pdf.

Greshko, Michael. "A Running List of How Trump Is Changing the Environment." National Geographic. May 10, 2017. http://news.nationalgeographic.com/2017/03/how-trump-is-changing-science-environment/#close.

Howard, Jordan, and Adora Svitak. *Green My Parents*. Santa Monica, CA: GreenMyParents, 2010.

"How Do Hybrid Cars and Trucks Work?" Union of Concerned Scientists. http://www.ucsusa.org/clean-vehicles/electric-vehicles/how-do-hybrids-work#.WSTLvVLMzm0.

"How Fossil Fuels Were Formed." US Department of Energy. http://www.fe.doe.gov/education/energylessons/coal/gen_howformed.html.

International Energy Agency. *The Evolving Renewable Energy Market*. Paris, France: 1999. p. v.

Jossi, Frank. "Minnesota Clean Energy Businesses Come Together to Lobby Legislature." Midwest Energy News. April 25, 2017. http://midwestenergynews.com/2017/04/25/minnesota-clean-energy-businesses-come-together-to-lobby-legislature.

Kiernan, John S. "2017's Greenest States." WalletHub. April 18, 2017. https://wallethub.com/edu/greenest-states/11987.

LaMonica, Martin. "Solar Junction Claims Cell Efficiency Record." CNet. April 14, 2011. https://www.cnet.com/news/solar-junction-claims-cell-efficiency-record.

Lipton, Eric. "Even in Coal Country, the Fight for an Industry." *New York Times*. May 29, 2012. http://www.nytimes.com/2012/05/30/business/energy-environment/even-in-kentucky-coal-industry-is-under-siege.html.

Maehlum, Mathias Aaree. "The History of Solar Energy." Energy Informative. August 14, 2013. http://energyinformative.org/the-history-of-solar-energy-timeline.

Martino, Justin. "Advancements in Wind Turbine Technology: Improving Efficiency and Reducing Cost." Power Engineering. March 14, 2014. http://www.power-eng.com/articles/print/volume-118/issue-3/features/advancements-in-wind-turbine-technology-improving-efficiency-and-reducing-cost.html.

Mavrokefalos, Anastassios, Sang Eon Han, Selcuk Yerci, et al. "Efficient Light Trapping in Inverted Nanopyramid Thin Crystalline Silicon Membranes for Solar Cell Applications." *NANO Letters*. Vol 12, Iss 6. May 2012. p. 2792–2796.

McCarthy, Joe. "7 Ways Obama Helped Protect the Planet from Climate Change." *Global Citizen*. January 18, 2017. https://www.globalcitizen.org/en/content/7-of-obamas-biggest-climate-change-victories.

Mooney, Chris. "Obama Has Done More to Save Energy Than Any Other President." *Washington Post*. August 5, 2016. https://www.washingtonpost.com/news/energy-environment/wp/2016/08/05/obama-has-done-more-to-save-energy-than-any-other-president/?utm_term=.9bcc8ba49d8e.

Morrison, Jim. "Air Pollution Goes Back Way Further Than You Think." Smithsonian.com. January 11, 2016. http://www.smithsonianmag.com/science-nature/air-pollution-goes-back-way-further-you-think-180957716.

Neville, Angela. "New Technologies Advance Biomass for Power Generation." *Power* magazine. July 1, 2012. http://www.powermag.com/new-technologies-advance-biomass-for-power-generation/?pagenum=1.

"New Drilling Technology Could Drive Advances in America's Geothermal Energy Industry." Office of Energy Efficiency and Renewable Energy. January 9, 2017. https://energy.gov/eere/articles/new-drilling-technology-could-drive-advances-america-s-geothermal-energy-industry.

Pruitt, Scott, and Luther Strange. "The Climate-Change Gang." *National Review*. May 17, 2016. http://www.nationalreview.com/article/435470/climate-change-attorneys-general.

Reilly, Michael. "Electric Cars Could Be Cheaper Than Internal Combustion by 2030." *MIT Technology Review*. May 23, 2017. https://www.technologyreview.com/s/607924/electric-cars-could-be-cheaper-than-internal-combustion-by-2030.

"Renewables 2016 Global Status Report." Renewable Energy Policy Network for the 21st Century. http://www.ren21.net/wp-content/uploads/2016/06/GSR_2016_Full_Report_REN21.pdf.

"Researchers Solve Mystery of Historic 1952 London Fog and Current Chinese Haze." Texas A&M Today. November 14, 2016. http://today.tamu.edu/2016/11/14/researchers-solve-mystery-of-historic-1952-london-fog-and-current-chinese-haze.

Rühle, Sven. "Tabulated Values of the Shockley-Queisser Limit for Single Junction Solar Cells." *Solar Energy*. Vol. 130. p. 139–147.

"Running on Renewable Energy, Burlington, Vermont Powers Green Movement Forward." PBS News Hour. January 31, 2015. http://www.pbs.org/newshour/bb/vermont-city-come-rely-100-percent-renewable-energy.

Sawin, Janet L. *Mainstreaming Renewable Energy in the 21st Century.* Worldwatch Paper 169. Washington, DC: Worldwatch Institute, May 2004.

Schipani, Vanessa. "The Facts on Trump's EPA Nominee." FactCheck.org. December 14, 2016. http://www.factcheck.org/2016/12/facts-trumps-epa-nominee.

"Solar." Institute for Energy Research. http://instituteforenergyresearch.org/topics/encyclopedia/solar.

"States Could Take Lead on Environmental Regulation Under Trump." NPR. January 18, 2017. http://www.npr.org/2017/01/18/510472419/states-could-take-lead-on-environmental-regulation-under-trump.

Thompson, Avery. "7 Ways to Power Your Home with Renewable Energy." *Popular Mechanics.* October 26, 2016. http://www.popularmechanics.com/science/energy/g2825/7-ways-to-power-your-home-with-renewable-energy.

Wald, Matthew L. "Court Overturns E.P.A.'s Biofuels Mandate." *New York Times.* January 25, 2013. http://www.nytimes.com/2013/01/26/business/energy-environment/court-overturns-epas-biofuels-mandate.html.

Wallace, Nick. "The Best Cities for Public Transportation." SmartAsset. February 24, 2016. https://smartasset.com/mortgage/best-cities-for-public-transportation.

Wang, Michael Q., Jeongwoo Han, Zia Haq, Wallace E. Tyner, et al. "Energy and Greenhouse Gas Emission Effects of Corn and Cellulosic Ethanol with Technology Improvements and Land Use Changes." *Biomass and Bioenergy.* Vol. 35, Issue 5. May 2011. Pgs. 1885–1896.

Woodard, Colin. "Maine Company Leading Way as Tidal Energy Comes of Age." *Portland Press Herald.* July 21, 2012. http://www.pressherald.com/2012/07/21/maine-company-leading-way-as-tidal-energy-comes-of-age_2012-07-22.

"World's First Triple Geo-PV-Solar Thermal Power Plant Unveiled in Nevada." *PV Magazine.* March 30, 2016. https://www.pv-magazine.com/2016/03/30/worlds-first-triple-geo-pv-solar-thermal-power-plant-unveiled-in-nevada_100023938.

You, Jingbi, Letian Dou, Ken Yoshimura, et al. "A Polymer Tandem Solar Cell with 10.6% Power Conversion Efficiency." *Nature Communications.* February 5, 2013.

Index

Page numbers in **boldface** are illustrations. Entries in **boldface** are glossary terms.

adaptive cells, 43
air conditioning, 61, 63, 94
air pollution, 14, 16–18, 20, **21**, 56, **58**, 59–60, 63, 71
Apple, 7, 76–77
Archimedian screw, 49–50

Becquerel, Edmund, 29
Bell, Alexander Graham, 19, 22–23
Bell Labs, 29, 40
bicylces, 69, 91, 93
biofuel, 24
biomass, 7, **36**, 55–56, 63, 72, 75
Block Island Wind Farm, 48
Bronze Age, 16
Brush, Charles, 27
businesses, 7, 24, 38, 51–56, 67–68, 70, 72–77, 79, 86

carbon dioxide, 5, 8, 24, 56, 63, 68, 73, 75, 81, 83, 86

cars, 7, 19, 23–25, 59, 63, **64**, 65–66–70, 81, **90**, 91–93, 95
Carter, Jimmy, 19
Chevrolet Volt, 66
Clean Air Act, 59, 80
Clean Power Plan, 83–84
climate change, 5, 7, 11, 18, 34, 56, 66–67, 69–70, 81, 83, 86–87, 89
coal, 5, 13–14, **15**, 16–17, 19–20, 22, 24, 44, 56, 63, 81, 83–84, **85**
coal gasification, 19
corn, 22–25
crude oil, 18, 65

dams, **8–9**, 26, 49, 52
deforestation, 11, 13
diesel, 19, 65–66, 92
district heating systems, 32–33
down conversion, 42–43
Drake, Edwin, 19
drilling, **10**, 19, 53–54
dye-sensitized solar cells, 41

108   Wind, Waves, and the Sun: The Rise of Alternative Energy

earthquakes, 33–34
electrical grid, 52, 61, 94
electric cars, 65–68, 70, 93
Energy, Department of, 7, 9, 14, 28, 45, 47, 49, 51, 54–55, 68, 70, 77, 83–84
energy-efficient mortgage (EEM), 70
Energy Star, 75, 94–95
enhanced geothermal systems (EGSs), 54–55
environmental impact, 19, 51–56, 60, 63, 69, 72, 91
Environmental Protection Agency (EPA), 7, 24, 59, 74–75, 77, 80, 84, 87, 94–95
ethanol, 23–25, 55

fines, 17
fish, 26, 52–53
floating wind turbines, 48
fog, 20, **21**
fossil fuel, 5, 7, 13–14, **15**, 16–20, 22–24, 30, 37, 44, 54, 56, 60, 63, 65, 72, 79, 81, 83–84, **85**, 87
fracking, 54
Fritts, Charles, 29
furnace, 60

garbage, 23, 56
gasoline, 18, 23–24
geothermal energy, **6**, 7–8, 32–34, 47, 53–55, 57, 63, 70, 74–75, 93–94
Geysers, The, 32–33
global warming, 5, 18, 56, 66–67, 86–87
Gore, Al, 74
greenhouse gases, 7, 23–24, 75, 83
GreenMyParents, 95

heating, 19, 29, 32–34, 38, 54–55, 60–61, 70, 72, 94
Hellenistic period, 24
homes, 7, 14, 16, 27, 30, 33, 38, 44, 55, 60–61, **62**, 63, 69–70, 72, 74, 79–80, **92**, 93–95
Honda Insight, 65
hybrid cars, 63, **64**, 65–66, 68, 70, 91
hydro energy, 7, **8–9**, **12**, 22, 24, 26, 47–53, 61, 63, 72, 75, 94
hydroEngine, 50
hydrogen-powered cars, 66, 68, 92
hydrokinetic, 51

Industrial Revolution, 16–17, 24, 27
Institute for Energy Research, 30, 48, 55
Intel, 74–75, 77

kerosene, 18–19
KidsEcoClub, 95
Kids FACE, 95
knots, 52
Kohl's, 75, 77

Larderello, 32–33
LEED, 71, 93
lessee, 72
lightbulbs, 27, 63
lignite, 16
lobby, 74
Lorax, The, 11, 13
Lukasiewicz, Ignacy, 18–19

mantle, 41
metrics, 71
Musk, Elon, 67

National Hockey League, 75
National Renewable Energy Laboratory, 9, 41, 46
natural gas, 5, 68, 86, 92
Neolithic period, 16
Niagara Falls, 26–27, **28**, 49

Nissan Leaf, 66
Nixon, Richard, 7
nuclear power, 5, 7, 54

Obama, Barack, 79, 81, **82**, 83, 86
Office of Energy Efficiency and Renewable Energy (EERE), 7, 47–48
offshore wind farms, 48
ovens, 29, 61, 94

Paleolithic period, 32
paraffin wax, 18
Paris Climate Agreement, 81, 83
peat, 16
perovskite, 41
petroleum, 5, 14, 18–19, 30
photon, 42–43
photovoltaics, 29–30, 38, 40–44, 54, 57, 61
pipe power, 53
polymer, 41
prisons, 72–73
Pruitt, Scott, 87
public transportation, 69, **88**, 91–93

rebates, 69–70
recidivism, 73

recycling, 73
refinery, 18–19
regulations, 17, 80–81, 83–84, 86
river currents, 52–53
Romm, Joseph, 68

Saussure, Horace Benedict de, 29
Schoellkopf, Jacob F., 26
schools, 29, 55, 73
semiconductor, 40–41
shingles, 60
Shuman, Frank, 30
silicon, 40
smog, **58**, 59–60
solar energy, **4**, 7, 9, 29–30, 32, 37–38, 40–44, **42**, 47–49, 54, 57, 60–61, 67, 70, 72–76, 79, **82, 90, 92**, 93–95
space exploration, 41, 67
steel, 46
Stillwater Geothermal Power Plant, 57
sugarcane, 23, 25
sulfur, 14, 20
Superfund site, 84
sustainable communities, 94

tax incentives, 69–70, 72–74
tectonic plates, 34
Tesla, 66–67
thin-film solar cells, 40–42
tidal power, 22, 47, 52
Toyota Prius, 65
Trump, Donald, 17, 70, **78**, 79, 83–84, 86–87
turbines, 27–29, **31**, 45–46, 48–53, 61, **62**, 80, 93

up conversion, 42–43
uranium, 5, 7

variable speed operation, 46
VIVACE, 52–53
vortices, 52–53

Walmart, 7, 75–76
Water Power Program, 49–51
wave power, 22, 47, 51–52
whale oil, 18
wind energy, 7, 9, 26–29, **31**, 32, 37–38, 44–48, 51, 61, **62**, 70, 72, 75, 80, 93
Wind Program, 45–46
wood, 11, 14, 18, 22, 60
Worldwatch Institute, 37, 44–47

Index 111

About the Author

Cathleen Small is the author of three dozen books on topics ranging from technology to biographies. Growing up in California in the 1970s and 1980s, Small was acutely aware of the environmental movement and has long been a supporter of eco-friendly living and green causes. In addition to being an author and editor, Small is cofounder of an award-winning grassroots advocacy coalition in California. When she's not writing, editing, or advocating, Small enjoys traveling with her husband, two young sons, and trusty pug.